NORMANDY

by CAMILLE MAUCLAIR

THE MEDICI SOCIETY

LONDON AND BOSTON

CONTENTS

Page

  I. Normandy : its History, Race, Character and Bounds.   9
 II. The Valley of the Seine, from the Epte to the Sea.   17
III. Upper Normandy, the District of Bray, Caux and the Seaside
        Resorts.   31
 IV. Rouen, Le Havre, Honfleur.   49
  V. Evreux, Lisieux, Pont-l'Evêque, the District of Auge, the
        Seaside Resorts from Honfleur to the Orne.   67
 VI. Caen, Bayeux, the Seaside Resorts from the Orne to
        Cherbourg.   81
VII. Cherbourg, the Cotentin, Coutances, Avranches.   99
VIII. Mont St-Michel.   115
 IX. Central Normandy and the Norman Switzerland.   127
  X. The Land, Feudal, Humanist and Christian.   149

Rouen. Court of the Palais de Justice.

In the Caux Country.

CHAPTER I
—

Normandy : Its History, Race, Character and Boundaries.

I like to hope that in this book the methods and qualities of a guide will not be expected of a writer who is a lover of art and nature. The scope of this slender volume would not admit of this; and hundreds of pages would hardly suffice if one desired to study, or even mention, all the notable buildings, all the resources and local characteristics of a region so rich in creative achievement, in varied scenery, in curiosities and memories accumulated throughout ten centuries. There are copious and well-arranged guide-books in existence, which have their own value and usefully achieve their object, which is to give minute

and exact information. But they only aim indirectly at arousing sentiment. And so in the present little work will be found above all things
the impressions, enthusiasms and suggestions of an artist taking a promenade through a countryside which contains much to admire, a
masterpiece of French order imposed upon French nature; of an artist
who has always believed that through love we achieve a higher understanding, and that one can only arouse love in others in so far as one
has experienced it oneself. If the sentiments expressed in the following
pages are communicable, the author's aim — namely, the " portrait of
a place " — will have been achieved and his highest desire realised.

And when we speak of a promenade, let us at once say that this
word should be taken in its literal sense, with its suggestion of leisure
and inconsequence. Those who travel by the great expresses, or even by
motor, may traverse Normandy, but they will not know it. In order to
savour its charm, and enter into its spirit, one must use the little departmental railways, or go by bicycle, country cart or boat. Above all, one
should tramp, without thinking about times and seasons, taking the sky
alone as one's counsellor from day to day. In this way one enjoys properly
the unspoilt pleasure of seeing this vast orchard dotted with charming
little towns. Normandy of the cornfields, the forests or the rivers is a land
for loitering in, where it is a joy to wander at large in a leisurely way,
like the gentle waters of the rivers and the slow procession of the clouds.

One can often distinguish a mysterious analogy, none the less real
for being incapable of proof, between the geographical configuration of
a country and its destiny. Let us look at the outline of Normandy on
the map. It bears a certain resemblance to that of a half-ruined fortress
with mighty foundations, built at the foot of the cliffs of Caux, and firmly
planted on the borders of old Brittany, with the worn battlements upon
its ramparts standing out against the sea, lifting up the Cotentin like a
proud watch-tower, in the face of England, while the foundations of this
castle, fissured by the Seine, rest upon the Ile-de France. This is no mere
geographical fancy. The fate of Normandy is summed up in full in this
outline, as clear in its symbolism as the Italian boot or the Scandinavian
lion. The destiny of Normandy was played out between England and the
Ile de-France, and the castle was subjected to innumerable assaults before
it could enjoy a definitive peace. Few lands have been so soaked in blood
as this. Fertile and smiling though it may be, the rivalry of those who
desired it was fierce. The traveller of to-day will perhaps care but little
for its history. But the memories of the past rise up before him too often
for him to be able to ignore it completely.

It was Caesar's legions who established the Gallo-Roman peace. The first martyrs for the Gospel were St. Nicaise and St. Honorin, whose work was carried on by St. Martin and St. Germain. With the Franks appeared the earliest monastic foundations, Saint-Pair, St-Evroult, St-Ouen, St-Wandrille and many others, up to the foundation of the abbey of Mont St. Michel at the beginning of the VIIIth century. A hundred years later came the Northmen, who spread from the Cotentin to the Seine, burnt Rouen, and threatened Paris with their flotillas, while at the same time the Bretons seized Avranches and pushed on as far as Bayeux. Reduced to impotence by the long struggle, Charles the Simple, who reigned at Paris, was forced to resign himself and cede to Rollo the Northman the territories from which he could not expel him, giving him his daughter's hand in the attempt to transform the invader into a satisfied vassal, if not into a friend and ally. The date 912 is that of the birth of Normandy. Once settled there, the Viking showed himself a hardy organiser of this fresh Neustrian duchy. He instituted order and discipline, and made his pirates, now contented colonists, adopt the Christian religion. But they did not renounce their taste for adventure. Having swarmed down from the Scandinavian North, they swarmed forth once more from the districts of Caux and the Bessin towards distant Italy, under the Dukes who succeeded Rollo, the three Richards and Robert the Magnificent, and enacted the amazing epic of the conquest of the peninsula and the Norman kingdom of the two Sicilies, with the brothers Guiscard. Even this great effort was not enough for them; nor was the task of consolidating their duchy against the attempts to recapture it of the earliest Capetians, alarmed at these energetic vassals so close at hand. A still larger swarm set out in quest of adventure, led by the relentless genius of the sixth duke, William the Bastard, a hundred and fifty years after the settlement of his ancestor, Rollo the Viking. William declared war on Harold, King of the Saxons and ruler of the Angles beyond the Channel. At Dives and Saint-Valéry he embarked two hundred and fifty thousand men on thousands of little ships; and, landing at Pevensey, he won the battle of Hastings, adding to his duchy of Normandy the kingdom of England.

This great historic feat was the beginning of the fierce struggle between the French monarchy and this menacing Anglo-Norman kingdom, which became still more acute when the Angevin Plantagenet married Eleanor of Aquitaine and found himself master of England, Normandy, Poitou and Aquitaine united, thus imperilling the prestige, and the very existence, of the Kings at Paris. Philip Augustus succeeded in severing this empire in two by conquering Evreux, Rouen and Normandy. Torn from the Angevins, she became thoroughly French in sentiment during the xiiith century, and turned into the lasting enemy of England, to which she had once sent forth her men. The Hundred Years' War made Normandy the battleground of the Anglo-French conflict, just as Lorraine has been in the wars between France and Germany. Again and again the Norman cities were besieged, sacked and burnt, after a heroic resistance, by the " godons ", men of Navarre, and the bands of whom Duguesclin was to clear the land. When, at the beginning of the xvth century, Henry V of England decided to lay claim to the crown of France, he desired first to regain possession of Normandy, whence sprang his race; and he stormed Harfleur, Caen and Rouen. The kingdom of Paris seemed to be lost, the conquest seemed final; and yet the national sentiment of Normandy had become so French that it resisted loyally. For thirty years they had to submit to the heavy domination of the English. It was at Rouen that Joan of Arc was burnt. But the awakening of France, which began at the siege of Orleans, gained ground, and at Formigny Charles VII's captains finally destroyed the last hopes of the intruders from beyond the Channel. Louis XI completed the task of attaching Normandy to the crown of France for good by suppressing the very title of the duchy. The memory of its origin and of the Anglo-Norman rivalries grew dim; and it was from the Norman coast, as well as from that of Brittany, that the boldest of the corsairs went forth, whether to fight their former English brother, now become the hereditary enemy, or to become his rival on the new trade routes to the Indies and Brazil. It was Francis I who created Le Havre in order to give wider scope to these brave sailors from Harfleur, Honfleur, Dieppe and Cherbourg.

When the Reformation arrived simultaneously with the Renaissance, Normandy was disturbed by it. Rouen and Caen opened their gates to Protestantism; the cruel Wars of Religion broke out; Coligny fought the royal armies in every part of the land; and fresh streams of blood were shed; till the victor of Arques, Henry IV, won over Normandy, with the rest of the kingdom, by abjuring Calvinism. A Jesuit reaction served the cause of absolute monarchy, which triumphed in the end. But many isolated Protestant groups continued to exist, which are still clearly perceptible to-day; and the ill-fated revocation of the Edict of Nantes was to impoverish the province by sending into exile the heads of its industry, which had been fostered by Colbert. Rising once more upon her ruins, Normandy, in spite of her loyalty, never ceased to lay claim to the maintenance of her old institutions and Estates; and she once more laid claim to them at the beginning of the Revolution. At first she favoured the Revolution, but, faced with the harsh centralisation of the Jacobins, she inclined towards federalism, though not daring to revolt entirely. But it was from Caen that Charlotte Corday set forth to assassinate Marat; and the Chouans of Brittany roved from Mortain to the Bocage and even as far as Caen. Far from revolutionary in temper, but desirous of peace and work, Normandy willingly accepted the Consulate and the Empire. But this was the end of her political activity; and after that she only regarded the successive governments with the semi-indifference of a race for which theories are of less importance than agricultural and economic problems. The long Anglo-Norman duel became no more than a memory; and the English now come with a pious and pacific curiosity to visit the castle at Falaise, which was William's cradle, Dives and Saint-Valéry, from whence his fleet set out, and the Bayeux Tapestry, which traces the stages of that Conquest from which was born modern England.

This rapid historical review is not concerned with things abstract and dead. The traveller is everywhere conscious of the sensation of a living past. These secular quarrels are related, not in the archives, but by the stones of abbeys and fortresses; and the very richness of the soil, its pastures, walled farms, orchards and forests, explains the bitter struggle to possess it, the persistent ebb and flow of the fratricidal combat between those who left the land to go beyond the seas, only to find, when they wished to return, that their former brothers had turned into enemies and allies of the crown of the Capets.

The race thus cleft in twain was a great race, if we cling to that notion which certain modern critics, out of opposition to the cut-and-dried affirmations of anthropology, have called " the prejudice of race ". The population of this vast region has been made up of successive immigrations of Ligurians, Celts, Romans, Saxons, Franks and Scandinavians; and when Rollo settled there, he was surrounded by a host of adventurers from every land. The union of all these elements was really consolidated when the duchy became French; and it became perfectly compact and homogeneous under the slowly modifying action of climate, out of the logical necessity arising from the character of the land itself, and obedience to the customs springing from this recognised necessity. Thus is created what we call a race, by the fusion of hordes of varied origin; race, which may be an anthropological fiction, but becomes a reality by the influence of soil and habitat.

The race which is called Norman has a double nature, formed by a perpetual process of oscillation. Morally, it was an off-shoot of the Nordic character, influenced by the genius of the Ile-de-France. Physically, it was attracted southwards by Paris, and northwards by the sea, from whence had sprung the hardy pirates who were the animating force among its primitive population. This race has been possessed by a violent passion for the rich soil of the land, which has rendered it provident and stay-at-home, economical and litigious — in fact, peasant in character. But it has been inspired by an equally violent passion for adventure, the hazards of the sea, and the great dreams of the ocean. These two passions have existed side by side. Within a very few miles the traveller may pass from the settled region of the home-loving population to the land from which set forth the pirates of Dieppe, rivals of the St. Malo corsairs, the conquistadors of Robert Guiscard, the discoverers of Canada and Brazil. And in this coast population, tall, fair and blue-eyed, the traveller will recognise the true Vikings or Northmen. The dark, squat men of the interior are more like the Normans of the glebe as popularised by Maupassant's realistic stories.

It is for the ethnologist to estimate the origins and proportions of these two contradictory factors. The traveller will avail himself of them in order to understand and relish better the character of those whom he will meet, in the absence of any knowledge of their patois. These must be spoken of in the plural, for there has never been, strictly speaking, a " Norman language "; but only a variety of local dialects. Of these the dialects of the coast regions have naturally preserved the linguistic traces of the Vikings better than the others; though the Northmen only formed a somewhat small nucleus among the numerous conquered populations. Their language is to be found in many names which have survived, and etymology points to many examples : the endings *bec*, meaning a streamlet (like the German *Bach*), *fleur* coming from *flodh* or *fleu* (a current), *dal* meaning valley (like the German *Thal*), *tot* meaning an open, grassy space, *beuf* or *bœuf* meaning, not a ruminating animal, but an improvised dwelling-place, an encampment, by a modification of the Nordic *bud*. Many others may be pointed out; *gard*, *hus*, *torp*, which are the English *house* and *garden* the German *Garten*, *Haus* and *Dorf*, the Dutch *huis* and *dort;* and finally *ham* (village) from which is derived the French *hameau* (hamlet) and which is so common in Picardy under the form *ham* or *hem*. In Normandy the persistence of Northern roots is visible more than elsewhere. These terms are combined with the ancient Gallic or Roman place-names : Veliocasses becoming Vexin, or Bajocasses Bayeux. The intruding pirates gave their own names to the places which they occupied, and their science of navigation supplied the subjugated coast population with many technical terms in use on the shores of the Baltic, in the straits of the Sound, and on the Norwegian, Saxon and Icelandic shores. But since the conquerors had started out like warriors on their rapid and perilous raids, bringing with them no female companions, they formed unions with the women of the occupied country; so that the Saxon dialects have left no trace in the interior, and the memory of them soon faded. It is the women who keep a language alive, and the children born of these unions with Gallo-Frankish women did not learn the Norse speech.

But if these questions are not to the traveller's taste — though they certainly have their interest — and he prefers simply to accept the Norman race as it is to-day, fused and unified by centuries of French influence, he will at least find in all he sees cause to admire the inventive genius of such a population. The most summary review of its history will inform him under what conditions of insecurity, continual alarms, burnings, pillage and slaughter, Normandy, whether Frankish, Angevin, or torn by the Hundred Years' War, went on steadily, with a splendid tenacity, building or restoring those innumerable cathedrals, abbeys, priories, fortresses or pleasure-houses which rise on every side among its woods and fields, and of which the xith century, above all, saw an amazing efflorescence. This genius for Romanesque architecture, to which was added the flower of Gothic, before the luxuriant bloom of the Renaissance, not only formed the proud adornment of Normandy, but crossed the sea at the time of William's conquests, and created the religious and seigniorial architecture of England. Such an achievement called for an inexhaustible fund of patience, steady energy and prudence, which form the very basis of the Norman character.

It is possible that, as people feared, the sudden penetration of the railways, which Normandy was the first to undergo, and the proximity of the Ile-de-France, due to this easy and rapid approach, have there, more than elsewhere, led to those dangers which the railway has everywhere introduced, side by side with its enormous benefits : I mean the sudden transformation of habits, the contagious vices of great cities, the abandonment of old customs, the abolition of the picturesque, of costumes, ornaments, fairs, river-navigation, the legends which sprang up in the long evenings, and the small local industries. The railways have been accused only too justly of being the death of old customs, and the propagators of centralisation, with its dull uniformity. Normandy is no longer as enthusiastic painters and writers depicted it half a century or more ago; and the popularity of its seaside resorts, into which Paris empties itself out, has largely contributed towards adulterating its ancient character. But its spirit remains alive, and it has its monuments and its landscapes, to which it is time to direct the traveller.

What are to be the limits of his domain? On the north and west the shores of the Channel, from Le Tréport to Mont St. Michel; from Picardy to Brittany by the estuary of the Seine, to the outpost of the Cotentin. On the south, from Mont St. Michel to Avranches, then to the outskirts of the Perche and Sarthe, Mortain, Domfront, Alençon, Verneuil, Evreux, Les Andelys and the line of the Epte; Gisors, Gournay and the land of Bray on the east, linking up with the district of the Somme. In it are comprised five departments, Seine-Inférieure, Eure, Orne, Calvados and Manche. But more real and more living than these administrative divisions, there remain the old regional appellations : Caux, Vexin, Roumois, Lieuvin, Ouche, Auge, Bessin, Cotentin, the Bocage; which evoke the memory of their towns and scenery. This immense orchard is divided into Upper and Lower Normandy by the lovely, winding Seine. There is no waterway of importance in Upper Normandy, hollowing out its way across the hard plateaux of the land of Caux; but the land west of the Seine is watered by the Eure, the Touque, the Dive, the Orne, the Odon, the Seulle, the Vire, the Sée, the Sélune, the Cance, the Risle.

Such is the setting for the " portrait of a region ", of which I shall attempt to sketch at least some of the features.

Normandy Fishers.

The Seine at Andelys.

CHAPTER II

—

The Valley of the Seine from the Epte to the Sea.

The traveller coming from the Ile-de-France, from Paris — that is to say, by the shortest way and the best train-service — has the choice of three routes, neatly spread out in the shape of a fan. The first is the one formerly followed by the " water coaches " or river diligences, the Valley of the Seine, Les Andelys, Rouen, Honfleur and Le Havre, from south to north, with the alternative of turning aside to the north-east, from Rouen to Dieppe, through Caux. The second route, from east to west, crosses Lower Normandy, through Evreux, Lisieux, Caen and Bayeux, turning north-west through the Cotentin to Cherbourg. The third route, also from east to west, goes from Dreux to Argentan, Vire, Granville or Mont St. Michel, leaving on its right, to the north, Falaise and Coutances, and on the left, to the south, Alençon, Domfront and Mortain. These three great arteries are linked up in between by a network of innocent little departmental trains, which dawdle along, catching connections at their own sweet will; and by roads so well kept up that they are inviting to carriages or pedestrians.

Entering Normandy by the first of these routes, one reaches the Epte after a charming journey through those most elegant suburbs which lie between Paris and Mantes; and one enters the French Vexin by way of La Roche-Guyon, Bonnières and Vernon, near which, at Giverny, is the fairy-like garden, which was the only luxury of the most illustrious of the impressionist painters, Claude Monet, who recently died there at the age of eighty-six. One of his most brilliant series of impressions is that of the Poplars on the Shores of the Epte. This little river forms the secular frontier between the Ile-de-France and Normandy; and the little village of St. Clair, through which it flows, is famous in history. It was there that in 912 Charles the Simple, King of Lutetia, unable to cope with the Vikings, resigned himself to treating with their leader Rollo, and in return for a purely formal vassalage, granted him the right of settling and creating the duchy of Normandy, from which, a century later, England was to spring. Henceforward the countryside became specifically Norman. The wooden houses with their exposed beams began to raise their high brown roofs against a background of sky and green hillside, and the Seine hollowed out a deeper bed between the wooded hills, scarred with quarries. The winding river advances for a time in a straight line, before yielding once more to its

Gisors. Ruins of the Dungeons.

love for those wide, meandering curves and loops which deflect its course seven or eight times before it reaches the sea. Ruined fortresses already tell of the bloody battles of the past, the merciless struggle for the possession of this fertile, happy country. Gisors, some way up the Epte on the right, is attractive, sweet and decked with flowers, and is commanded by the ruins of a formidable keep, built for the son of the Conqueror, taken by the English and retaken by Charles VII, which still raises proudly aloft these mighty remains of the military architecture

Gisors. Ruins of the Dungeons.

of the Middle Ages, among the trees of a noble park. Gisors points the way to the district of Bray, where we shall go later. But on the left bank, quite near the river, is Gaillon. There, on the site of a Gallo-Roman fort, the genius of the Renaissance, at the behest of the Cardinal d'Amboise, built a wondrous pleasure-house, carved by Michel Colombe and Juste de Tours, of which the Ecole des Beaux-Arts and the Louvre in Paris preserve such fine fragments. Louviers, on the Eure, before it became a peaceful industrial city, enriched by its cloth manufactures — Louviers, the ancient Loveris, to which the humanists gave the name of *Locus Veris*, the Abode of Spring — was taken by the English, but drove them out during the great final effort for the liberation of Normandy. It was taken later on by the Protestants, then by the troops of the League, then by Henry IV, so that it is far from being one of those cities which have not

Château Gaillard.

experienced several times the horrors of assault, pillage, massacre and fire. This was the destiny of Pont-de-l'Arche, where Charles the Bald had ordered a palace to be built near the bridge, and where the abbey of Bon Port was created as the result of a vow made by Richard of the Lion Heart. Everything in this region was an advanced outpost of the Ile-de-France against her redoubtable Nordic neighbours. But Les Andelys will furnish us with the most striking example of this warlike function.

The Seine leads us by a great bend, betwen high limestone cliffs crowned with verdure, to these two little twin towns. Le Grand Andelys is the more ancient of them. Queen Clotilde founded a monastery there; it was captured by Louis the Fat and recaptured by Richard of the Lion

Louviers. Church of Notre-Dame.

The Seine from Château-Gaillard.

Heart, who wished to make it one of the keys of his duchy. He chose the rock commanding the Seine, and built on it an impregnable fortress, the Château Gaillard. At the foot of this fortress clustered the church and houses of a fresh nucleus, Le Petit Andelys. Many dramatic events took place there. This eagle's nest withstood many a determined attack.

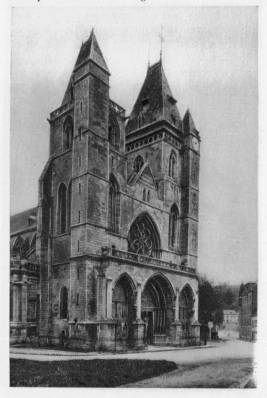

Church of Le Grand-Andelys.

It took Philip Augustus five months to take it from John Lackland. Henry V of England recaptured it, Charles VII took possession of it King Antony of Navarre came there to die of his wounds, Margaret of Burgundy was strangled there. Henry IV at last had it dismantled, and Richelieu finished the task of effacing these tragic memories by reducing the keep to ruins. The remains of its three enceintes are still formidable, with their walls nine and twelve feet thick, isolated by triple moats hewn in the rock. The horror of assaults and tortures has faded away, and nothing remains, after a rough ascent, save the joy of a magnificent landscape, a view embracing the river and its islands, and the French and Norman countryside, doubly commanded by the redoubtable stony mass full of men-at-arms.

The capricious windings of the Seine next lead us to Pitres or Pistres, another old residence of Charles the Bald, where he summoned councils, and decided to fortify all the high places of the land against the growing peril of the Northmen. Pitres is built at the confluence of the Seine and the pretty Andelle, where it issues from a charming valley, full of villages dear to landscape painters — Fleury, Charleval and Radepont, with its ruined fortress. On the east, this valley leads up to the deep Forest of Lyons, one of the most attractive in France. Above Pitres rises the celebrated hill of the Deux Amants (Two Lovers), with its significant profile and touching legend. A young knight was in love with the beautiful daughter of a lord of this land. " My daughter shall be yours, " he declared, " if you can carry her in your arms up to the summit of the cliff without resting a single moment ". The knight lifted his beloved in his arms and began the ascent. By a mighty effort he succeeded in reaching the top, but there his heart broke, he laid down his precious burden, and fell down dead. The lady, distraught, seized in her turn the body of him who had just died for love of her, and threw herself with it into the abyss, before the eyes of the cruel father and the terror-stricken crowd. This beautiful story of faithful love and a pathetic death, which makes one think of that of Tristan and Isolde, has not been forgotten, and it must often have been repeated with embellishments during those long evenings in Normandy, the tradition of which is gradually dying out; for people no longer weave or spin at home of an evening. Factories and stock-breeding

Les Andelys. Old houses and ruins of Château Gaillard.

Croisset. Pavillon Flaubert.

have killed these old-fashioned evenings, during which legends were handed down.

We soon come to an example of this on arriving at Elbeuf, meanly situated and artistically poor. From the Middle Ages to the days of Colbert it was a city famous for its prosperous cloth factories. The ill-starred revocation of the Edict of Nantes almost ruined it. It recovered, none the less, after the Revolution, but all the ancient methods have been transformed. The famous " elbeufs ", beloved of the middle classes — for they wore for ever — were formerly woven at home; and where they did not use those antiquated spinning-wheels which now serve no purpose save to adorn our museums and drawing-rooms, hand-looms were set up in every country cottage. People could then work during their evenings, conversing the while. But now factories have come, and the field labourer has left his rustic home to become a suburban factory-hand. Elsewhere, arable land is shrinking and is replaced by stock-breeding, which pays better and is not such hard

Griffon of Saint-Wandrille.

Abbey of Jumièges.

Cloister of Saint-Wandrille.

work. This is yet another reason why the preservation of traditions is being lost with the long evenings at home.

We are now in the very heart of Norman territory, in the Roumois; and its capital, Rouen, is not far distant. We will just pass by, and return there at leisure. The lovely river carries us along, winding more wilfully than ever, and in order to admire its windings the better, we can go by boat. For though the railway has superseded the " water coaches ", pleasure boats still exist, and even commercial navigation is by no means extinct — witness the unending procession of barges along the Seine as it descends to the sea like a trium-

phal avenue. The scenery of both banks becomes still finer. Each of the five great loops which we pass, one after the other, like the coils of some glittering serpent, reveals the billowing leafage of a great forest : the Forest of Le Rouvray, the Forest of Roumare, the Forest of Mauny, the Forest of Jumièges, the Forest of Brotonne, outlined by the babbling waters, and facing each other on opposite banks of the stream, studded with islands, which rolls on its way through verdant meadows at the foot of hills covered by venerable woodlands. It is one of the sights of

Old Wells at Jumièges.

the purest beauty in the sweet land of France.

On leaving Rouen, we first make a respectful halt before the simple little xviiith century dwelling, hardly larger than one big room, and surrounded by a simple garden, which rises upon the cliffs at Croisset. It was here that Gustave Flaubert, toiling at his ascetic task, completed his immortal work and meditated in haughty pessimism. It was here that death surprised him at his writing-table, which has been piously preserved with all the furnishings which he used day by day. Further on, at the foot of the cliffs, crowned, at a height of about three hundred feet, by the woods of La Londe, we may have a plentiful lunch of *matelote*

Cloister of Saint-Wandrille.

(fish stew) or fried fish at one of the inns of that amusing spot La Bouille, to which so many trippers go from Rouen, where so many tourists stop, and which was once a regular port. But soon a triple bend in the river brings us past Jumièges and Saint Wandrille. Jumièges, an abbey founded in the viith century by Saint Philbert, has its famous, though dubious, legend of the *Enervés*. According to some accounts, the Benedictines took in, at the point of death, two sons of Clovis II, who had been turned adrift in a boat to float downstream, with the muscles (nerfs) of their legs severed, for rebelling against their mother, Bathilde. According to others, it happened to two Dukes of Bavaria, said to have been punished in this way by Charlemagne. Charles VII often came to the abbey with Agnès Sorel, who bequeathed her heart to it. No words can express the emotion of exalted melancholy which one feels, particularly at twilight, surrounded by great trees, among these majestic ruins, before the portal commanded by two massive octagonal towers, fifty yards high, the roofless nave, the Gothic arch which still supports a part of the central tower, the side-chapels, through the breaches of which pierce the sun's dying rays, the chapter-house, the crypt, the whole framework of this colossal stone structure built by genius for the exaltation of faith, destroyed by the centuries, deserted by man, yet still capable of stirring the soul to ardent prayer. Saint-Wandrille is on a far smaller scale and does not produce the same overwhelming impression. But it is a delightful spot, a " refuge of peace ", in which life is still going on. In the middle of the viith century it was founded by a disciple of St. Columban, Wadregisille or Wandrille, and it flourished and was venerated as a Benedictine abbey. It then declined and began to crumble away, till in the xviith century the Benedictines of St. Maur attempted to restore it. After the

Saint-Wandrille. Ruins of the Abbey.

Revolution a cotton-mill was set up in it; then the Benedictines returned once more. The law relating to religious bodies has lately driven them out, and the abbey has been let to private persons. The buildings added in the xviith century are still habitable, and harmonise well with the Gothic halls, the old refectory — half Gothic, half Renaissance — the cloister filled with tombs and statues, and the remains of the abbey church.

The sunk garden, with its pool and its yew-trees, is wonderfully graceful, and on all sides trees, water, ivy and flowers unite with the stone, the light and the silence to compose in this spot the most perfect, touching poem of art, piety and nature.

After this double vision of the Middle Ages, " enormous yet delicate ", comes the picturesque apparition of the little old town of Caudebec, a river-port, yet already a sea-port, once the capital of Caux, with its ancient houses, its fine church of Notre-Dame in the flamboyant style, the spire of which rises above a most animated harbour. If we arrive at the right moment, the day after the new moon, we shall see the harbour swept by the tumultuous in-rush of a wave three hundred yards long. It is the bore, or *masca-ret*, the irresistible tidal wave, the clash between the current of the river flowing sea-ward and the pressure of the neighbouring sea, as the tide flows up from Le Havre to the interior of Normandy. At the season of the equinox, in particular, it is an imposing sight. From this point onwards the life of the river is at an end; though the Channel is still invisible, and the Seine has not yet widened out into an estuary. Here is Villequier, where Victor Hugo's daughter perished with her husband; Lillebonne, the Roman Juliobona, where we may still see a great

Harfleur.

ancient theatre, and a fortress of William the Conqueror; Tancarville, dominated by a manor-house, which has been inhabited and transformed since the xth century by a long series of owners bearing the greatest names of France; and lastly, Harfleur, with its pretty, flamboyant church — Harfleur, which for long stoutly withstood the English and equipped pirates to attack them, but fell from its high estate as its harbour became more and more paralysed and silted up with sand, and, finally, when Le Havre was founded.

Now we have the estuary and the sea. Its mighty breath could already be felt as soon as we passed the point of Quillebeuf on the opposite shore. Between Tancarville and La Roque the shores are scooped out and become coasts, a great harbour is hollowed out between Harfleur and Honfleur, and the Seine proudly yields herself up and mingles with the sea, dying in a transfiguring blaze of light.

Cloister of Saint-Wandrille.

Château of Mesnières.

—

CHAPTER III

Upper Normandy, the District of Bray,
Caux and its Seaside Places.

From Rouen we may well turn our course towards the land of Caux, which forms, with the district of Bray, what has been called Upper Normandy, to the north and east of the Seine. The limestone plateaux of Caux begin to overhang the east bank of the river, and extend as far as the sea. This region is swept by boisterous winds. It was the first land occupied by Rollo's adventurers, before they annexed territories on the left bank, and boldly descended through the Vexin to Paris, from whose walls the courage of Count Odo and the mystical fortitude of St. Geneviève had succeeded in repelling their forbears on a previous occasion. Before preparing to travel through Caux, perhaps it would be best to traverse the outskirts of Normandy, through Bray, which borders upon Picardy. We can reach it by way of the valley of the Epte, from Vernon to Gisors, or from Pitres, by the soft valley of the Andelle, which flows round the luxuriant Forest of Lyons. Both of these ways lead to Gournay, which is a pleasant, quiet little town, with its old Romanesque and Gothic church of St. Hildevert and, near by, the ancient abbey of St. Germier, whose half ruined nave is still most valuable for the study of the earliest Gothic. We are at the very edge of the Oise country, the Beauvaisis, in that district

Peasant's House near Bray.

of Formerie where the amazing little citadel of Gerberoy, now reduced to some hundred inhabitants, rises upon a hill. It is the very type of the forts constructed throughout all this region of the marches as a check upon the English. It was here that the brave La Hire defeated the Earl of Arundel. It was burnt by the League. After this the town fell into a delightful sleepy silence, its crumbling ramparts succumbed to the attacks of all kinds of vegetation, and this warlike stronghold turned into that rustic, flower-grown poem which inspired the fine canvasses of the painter Le Sidaner, that faithful, pensive guest of Gerberoy. If we are disinclined to cross the imaginary frontier separating Normandy from the Beauvaisis, we turn towards the left, and, passing the prettily bedecked watering-place of Forges-les-Eaux, we arrive at Neufchâtel-en-Bray, where Colonel Driant, one of the heroes of Verdun, was

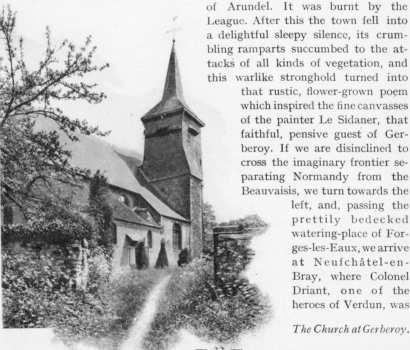

The Church at Gerberoy.

— 32 —

Gerberoy. The Environs.

born, and whose castle, built by Henry I of Normandy and England, was often taken and retaken before it was dismantled by Henry IV, the chief destroyer of castles before Richelieu. All these Norman castles were built by royal order, for or against the English, and condemned by royal order after hard and loyal use, when the united monarchy could see in them nothing but the haunts of rebel barons, or simply the last vestiges of feudal independence. All that they spared were the harmless pleasure-houses with which the smiling genius of the Renaissance covered the territory of France. One of the finest witnesses of this is the chateau of Mesnières, near Neufchâtel. At the gates of Dieppe, another imposing building recalls, on the other hand, the struggles of the past. It is the fortress of Arques, built by the uncle of the Conqueror, which saw within its walls Philip Augustus and St. Louis; which the English took by storm after capturing Rouen, and, finally, beneath which Henry IV, contesting his future kingdom with the Duke of Mayenne, won, after Ivry and Fontaine-Françoise, the decisive battle which gained him the crown. In the xviiith century the deserted castle gradually crumbled away. First private individuals, then nuns, took its stones to rebuild their houses or convents and it was not till late that the

Arques. The Church.

State acquired the remains of this noble ruin in order to preserve it. It is near a charming church, whose rood-screen is a masterpiece. And from the rounded hill on which the castle stands one has a view from the deep Forest of Arques to the sea by Dieppe, and the valley of the Eaulne, over a landscape whose rich colour and the beauty of its varying planes

Rood Screen at Arques.

are hardly surpassed by anything in Normandy, except the views from Avranches, Mortain and Domfront.

Turning north-eastwards from Neufchâtel, the line of the river Bresle, which separates the district of Bray from the plateau of Vimeu, will lead us to Aumale. This is another very ancient little Norman city, which has seen many a fight. William Rufus, one of the Conqueror's sons, took it in the xiith century, and Charles the Bold in the xvth century. Three years after his triumph over the League at Arques, Henry IV nearly lost his fortune and his life here in a bloody encounter with the Spaniards, in which he was defeated and wounded.

Following the course of the Bresle, we shall soon arrive at Eu, the Roman Aucum, across the verdant countryside of Vimeu, the character of which is already Picard rather than Norman. Eu is a town full of noble and tragic memories. It was while defending its castle that Rollo was slain It was in this castle, founded in Carlovingian days, that the Conqueror was betrothed to Matilda and had that interview with Harold which led to his

Rood Screen at Arques.

Eu. The Château.

English expedition. It was here, too, that Joan of Arc was taken prisoner on that sad journey which brought her from Compiègne to Rouen. In the xvith century a magnificent pleasure-house was built there by the Guises on the site of the old fortress; and in the following century Mademoiselle de Montpensier created the park. Eu became the property of the Orleans family. The Revolution and the fire of 1902 once more transformed the aspect of this fine estate, but restoration has always resolutely kept pace with ruin, and Louis Philippe, in particular, took a fancy to Eu and carried out great works there, making it his favourite residence, in which he twice entertained Queen Victoria. Near by the castle, between the forest and the region

Lake at Forges-les-Eaux.

bordering on Le Tréport and the sea, the little city, which now seems so calm, has suffered much in past days. It was entirely burnt by order of Louis XI, and besieged by the Protestants of Dieppe; and during that desperate struggle which was soon to be ended by the victory of Arques the same week saw it captured by Henry IV and recaptured by Mayenne.

In far distant days the town of Eu, so proud of its splendid park, its fine church of St. Laurent and its royal guests, was a port. But since the xɪth century, the gradual silting up of the coast led to the creation of the new port. This was Le Tréport, towards which the Counts of Eu diverted the lower course of the Bresle. Le Tréport (the harbour on the other side of Eu), on the left bank of the Bresle, is the last town in the region of Caux and the department of Seine-Inférieure. On the right bank, the recently-created watering-place of Mers marks the beginning of

Eu. The Church.

Picardy and the department of Somme. Le Tréport, too, fought bravely against the English invaders, and the Protestants reduced its old church, perched upon the cliffs, to ruins, only to rebuild it. It is a picturesque spot, with pretty outlines, to which great animation is lent by a considerable fleet of fishing and coasting boats. From above, on the terraces overlooking the port, there is one of the finest views along the Channel coast, towards Dieppe, the Somme and the open sea. But the life of the sailors and shipping is nothing compared to the crowds poured out by the numerous trains from Paris — especially from Saturday to Monday — a crowd of townspeople eager to breathe the sea air for a while, a noisy, plebeian crowd, transported there in a few hours, at moderate rates, which swarms

The Port of Dieppe.

all over this extensive region, infecting it with its own vulgarity.

There is little inducement to return into the interior of the district of Caux, save to draw attention to Yvetot, which would be of no interest without its gay legend of the " King ", spread by the jests of Henry IV, the songs of Béranger and the operetta called " Le Roi d'Yvetot ". It has some basis of fact, for in the xvth century the lords of this place really had that title. All the same, it is the original nucleus of old Normandy, the first settlement of the Northmen, and the Cauchois, or inhabitants of Caux, have jealously preserved the character and customs of the past, longer than all the other inhabitants of the province, whether inland or

Yvetot.

along the coast. As in former days, they live scattered about the
countryside in isolated farms, often at some distance from each other,
sheltered by a screen of fine trees. It is in this region, where stone is scarce
and wood abundant, that, as in the neighbourhood of Lisieux, we find
the typical style of " Norman " house, as it is called, with its wooden
frame exposed and painted, framing the white roughcast beneath high

Dieppe. General View of the Sea Front.

gables. Caux is a rich agricultural district, entirely peasant in character.
It gradually rises in a gentle slope as far as the Channel coast, where it
suddenly breaks off, raising above the shore its perpendicular granite
cliffs, like a high wall, sometimes rising to a height of 300 feet. From
time to time this wall is cut by a little waterless valley, in the hollow
of which hides a village. Such is the general character of that part of
the coast which extends from Le Tréport to Le Havre, and to which
the comparatively recent fashion for staying at the seaside, which was
formerly deserted, or left to the fisherfolk, has given a life, character and
appearance unknown till the xixth century. It is as if the sea had made
a violent cleavage of the land, as with an axe, laying bare below the
surface soil and chalk the stony skeleton of the plateau of Caux. A few
steps, and we pass without transition from the pastures full of cattle to
the vast expanse of the sea.

Manoir d'Ango.

Such is, in brief, the general character of this coast, by which we shall complete the circuit of Caux along the top of the cliffs. We shall find a series of watering-places, most of which have transformed humble seaside villages beyond recognition by the addition of a new quarter with all the resources of modern comfort, often to the detriment of their picturesqueness. Our forefathers had no desire for sea-bathing, maintaining before the terrible ocean either a state of indifference, or a survival of the horror of sea and mountain professed by the ancient world, with no idea of finding beauty in it, still less of using it as an aid to hygiene. Though most places in Caux adorn their names with the proud suffix " ville ", they are mere villages or hamlets. We need only draw attention to the fine chateau of Miromesnil, not far from Dieppe, where Maupassant was born. The real life of this region nowa-

A Column at the Manoir d'Ango.

Fécamp. Boats in port.

Saint-Valéry-en-Caux. The Market Place.

days is in these watering-places ranged along the coast on both sides of Dieppe, which one reaches from Le Tréport by way of Mesnil-Val, Criel, Berneval and Puys, all quiet seaside places. Dieppe has a very fine history, dating from the xiith century, when the depth of its harbour enabled it to play an important part, which the kings of France appreciated, and therefore encouraged the city. From Dieppe, as from Saint Malo, for many centuries those bold captains set out, who hunted the English ships up and down the Channel But Dieppe did not only nurture pirates; it also sent forth explorers, as intrepid and experienced as the ancient Vikings, who ventured as far as Cape Verde. One of the most famous was Ango, who at the beginning of the xvith century, having seen his ships captured

Fécamp. Courtyard of the Abbey.

and pillaged by the Portuguese, ventured to send a flotilla to lay waste the cities of Portugal, threatening Lisbon, and forcing the king to compensate them for their ships. This Ango was a great ship-builder and was encouraged and worthily rewarded by Francis I, who protected and enlarged Dieppe. He was a powerful ship-builder; and his manor, which can still be visited near Varangeville, was that of a regular seigneur living in luxury and loving beautiful things, as is shown by the rich and delicate carvings of his great house. Dieppe was at the same time a fortress and a fishing-port, which sent ships to the cod-fisheries as far as Norway and Iceland. So the little city was rich and animated, and its tradesmen managed to make it one of the most frequented markets in the north of France.

It was the men of Dieppe who at the beginning of the xivth century seized Southampton,

Fécamp. Courtyard of the Abbey.

and in later days had a share in the naval victory of La Rochelle. The English hated them; and after the great disaster of Agincourt in 1415, broke into Dieppe and treated it cruelly. But fifteen years later, the inhabitants managed to recapture the town while Caux rose against the foreigners; and they built the castle which still commands the sea. Other trials were in keeping for Dieppe after the age of Francis I, during which she was so flourishing. There were the Wars of Religion, during which Normandy was laid waste; and part of the struggle between the League, the Spaniards and Henry IV was carried on, with all its fluctuations, in Caux at the very gates of Dieppe. There was the plague of 1668-1670, which killed ten thousand persons. There was the ill-fated revocation of the Edict of Nantes, which drove so many useful citizens into exile. Fi-

nally, there was the severe bombard-ment by the An-glo-Dutch fleets in 1694, which almost destroyed the town which had given birth to the glorious Duquesne Dieppe was slow to recover. It needed the fash-ion for sea - bath-ing, introduced at Dieppe by the Du-chess of Berry, to restore its pros-perity in the xixth century, aided by the construction of railways, which brought it rapid communication with Rouen and Paris, and its selec-tion as the port of departure for the Newhaven steam-boats. During the war, Dieppe was

The Cliffs at Etretat.

an important English base. Though its glorious past is at an end, it still remains a pleasant and very lively centre for sea-bathing, besides its considerable importance as a commercial port, with its pretty church of St. Jacques, its picturesque feudal castle, its shops full of carved ivory and laces, and its fine promenade along the sea-front.

The Cliffs at Etretat.

Along the cliffs from Dieppe to Le Havre runs a series of places whose fortune has been made by the fashion for sea-bathing, and where Claude Monet has painted a number of his finest pictures : Pourville, Varangeville with its church standing alone on the edge of a precipitous rocky plateau, the lighthouse of Ailly, Quiberville and Saint-Aubin-sur-Dun, Veules-les-Roses, Saint-Valéry-en-Caux, founded by the saint, it is said, at the same time as Saint-Valéry-sur-Somme, Veulettes at the mouth of the Durdent, Les Petites Dalles and Les Grandes Dalles, Saint-Pierre-en-Port, Sonneville. And here is Fécamp, with its beautiful, mysterious legend, which alleges that in the first century a boat

Bas-relief in the Church of Biville-sur-Mer.

went ashore there, made of the hollowed trunk of a fig-tree, containing in a leaden box a few drops of the blood of Christ collected by Joseph of Arimathea. This belief gave rise to a pilgrimage, a convent of nuns, which was sacked by the Northmen, and later a Benedictine abbey, whose fortune and power were increased by the fame and profits from the famous liqueur Bénédictine, and never ceased to grow, in spite of the attacks of the English during the Hundred Years' War, until the Revolution, which overthrew the abbey, but left untouched the precious relic, the Grail of Normandy. The buildings once inhabited by the monks have long since been turned to other uses; but the great abbey church of La Trinité, though its front was rebuilt in the xviiith century, and two of its towers are lacking, still stands as a magnificent example of the beginnings of Norman Gothic in the xith and xiith centuries. This rude but powerful style is seen side by side with the delicate chapels of Renaissance inspiration which are to be found inside the church. Around this august spot had grown up a little city. Its excellent harbour, running deep inland between two hills, can hold a considerable fishing-fleet, which goes to the cod-fisheries of Newfoundland and Iceland, visiting the herring and mackerel fisheries on the way back. Fécamp is also a pleasant seaside place, and there is still a Bénédictine distillery; for though the monks have disappeared, their recipes are left. In the little cemetery above the town, in accordance with his last wishes. lies, like a faithful son of Fécamp, the only writer whom the town has produced, the novelist Jean Lorrain, who did not do himself full justice, but whose incisive talent places him among the most remarkable prose-writers of Normandy.

Church of Montivilliers.

After Yport, Vaucottes with its impressive cliffs, Benouville with its valleys hollowed out in the living rock, and the Aiguille de Belval standing in isolation in the sea, for ever assailed by the waves, there appears one of the most famous and picturesque watering-places of the Channel coast, Etretat, once a simple fishing-village, where Isabey the younger, and afterwards Le Poittevin, painted their marine landscapes, and which Alphonse Karr and afterwards Maupassant brought into fashion. The little city is huddled on the edge of a rather narrow shingly beach, the curve of which is bounded by the two celebrated cliffs, the Falaises d'Amont and d'Aval, which produce such a grand impression. Hollowed into caves in which the waves break at high tide with a tragic moaning, these cliffs are unique. The Falaise

The Woods of Yport.

d'Aval, in particular, is pierced by a natural arch, the work of the waves, whose capricious action has pointed it like a Gothic doorway. Before it stands the pointed monolith, called the Needle, rising to a height of 230 feet above the surrounding water. Beyond it is yet another arch, the *magna porta* or Manneporte, the top of which reaches a height of 295 feet. Passing by these wonderful and imposing sights, and continuing westwards, enjoying all the time a magical view over the coast, the country and the high seas, we arrive at that vast accumulation of white rocks and red soil which composes the cape of Antifer, 360 feet high, forming the pedestal of a mighty lighthouse. In places such as this, Normandy is not merely a pleasant, verdant land, but takes on a pathetic majesty, as her soil rears itself against the fury of the sea. This character persists, though in a softer form, at Bruneval and Saint Jouin, a charming, flowery spot where the traveller finds waiting for him the famous Hôtel de la Belle Ernestine, enriched with a little museum, where pictures by famous artists are found side by side with a valuable series of autographs, accumulated during sixty years by the writers who have stayed at this hospitable house. During the war these were increased by the signatures and remarks of English generals and the members of the heroic Belgian Government, who had found a temporary home at Saint-Adresse and along the coast. After snatching a few hours to turn aside from Octeville and its cliffs and pay a rapid visit to the old abbey of Montivilliers, founded in the viith century by Saint Philbert, the creator of Jumièges, we come in sight of the cape of La Hève, with its promontory 345 feet high, and its brilliant lighthouses sending out their beams over a radius of fifty miles. From here in clear weather we can see the point of the Cotentin, shimmering in the light reflected from the sea; and at our feet lie Le Havre and the estuary of the Seine.

Yport. Fishing Boats.

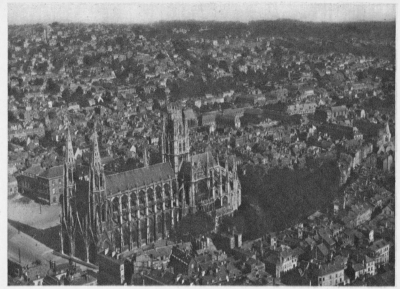

General View of Rouen.

—

CHAPTER IV

Rouen, Le Havre, Honfleur

Rouen, the queen of Gothic Normandy and one of the great French princesses of beauty, appears in all its stately grace when we look down upon it from the extremity of the hill of Bon Secours, which commands the Seine, a vast expanse of meadow-land, the forests and the whole city, with its innumerable church-towers, above which soars the lofty spire of the cathedral. No town could be dearer to the heart of an artist or historian in search of the memories and emotions of a great past.

The splendour of Rouen has often been threatened, like all the beauties of this rich land of Normandy. The first bishops of the

Hôtel Bourgtheroulde.
(Detail).

ancient Gallic and Roman Rotomagus were destined to become saints, like Mello, Ouen and Romain, or were worthy to do so — for instance Praetextatus, whom Fredegond caused to be stabbed at the altar. Rouen was taken and sacked by the Viking Ogier the Dane, before Rollo settled there and made it the capital of his duchy. Philip Augustus took Rouen. Under Charles VI it was recaptured by the English, after one of the most terrible sieges in all European history, when ten thousand " useless mouths, " old men, women and children, died of starvation at the foot of the ramparts, between the besieged, who had shut them out, and the besiegers who drove them back. The Place du Vieux Marché, which has become one of the Holy Places of France, was the scene of the unforgettable crime of the French ecclesiastical judges, abettors of the hate of the English — namely, the death of the heroic maid Joan of Arc. Eleven years later, Dunois forced Talbot to yield up the city, which had risen against the oppressor, with the rest of Normandy, in a great upheaval which threw the English armies back to the sea for good. The Wars of Religion caused Rouen to be subjected to two fierce sieges. It was taken by the Protestants and reoccupied by the Catholics, and suffered pillage and massacre, before enjoying that long peace which was only broken by the humiliating Prussian occupation in 1870. It is a very rich town, a great port, an enormous centre of cotton-spinning, from which go forth thousands of tons of those " Rouenneries " which are known throughout the whole world. But the clean, agreeable, luxu-

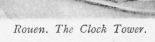

Rouen. The Clock Tower.

rious, modern city has grown up round the original nucleus without altering it. In the heart of modern Rouen old Rouen remains untouched, crowding its marvels into a somewhat narrow space.

They have been so much celebrated that all attempts at description are discouraged from the outset. One must pause in a spirit of simplicity, content with the joys of love and admiration, before this group of monuments, which, if

Hôtel Bourgtheroulde.

they alone were to survive some universal cataclysm, would suffice to bear witness to the grandeur of human genius in the Gothic age and at the Renaissance. A harmony as strong and subtle as that of a symphony makes itself felt in the structure of Louis XII's Palais de Justice, with its splendid stone hall known as the Salle des Pas Perdus and its noble, ample façade which blooms into the delicate carving of the balconies, the window-frames, the chimneys and gargoyles. The Hôtel Bourgtheroulde is a gem, with its bas-reliefs representing so ingeniously the Triumphs of Petrarch. The Grosse Horloge is another, that amazing group composed of a clock-tower, a fountain and an arch, in whose composition and fantastic ornament, exquisitely mellowed by time, are concentrated all the graces of Gothic and Renaissance art, as they were understood in Normandy. The lover of art will complete his enjoyment of these masterpieces by a visit to the museum of antiquities,

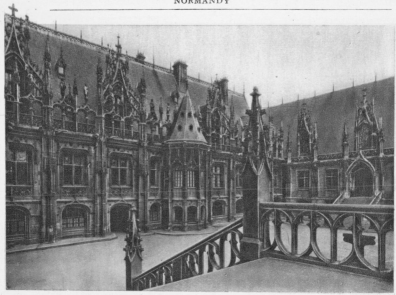

Rouen. Courtyard of the Palais de Justice.

whose treasures would make all the antiquaries in the world sick with envy, and where the history of Normandy, since Merovingian days, is sumptuously set forth in pictures and relics. The museum of the Fine Arts is one of the most intensely interesting in provincial France. Its grand staircase boasts a fresco by Puvis de Chavannes, and its galleries abound in works of the highest merit, Italian, Dutch and French. It has a marvellous Gérard David, a predella by Perugino, David's portrait of Madame Vigée-Lebrun, the " Belle Zélie " of Ingres, some proud Largillières, some Ruysdaels and Van Goyens. Its modern rooms contain, among others, pictures by Ziem, Courbet, Daubigny and Corot. Here is the touching little *Retreat from Russia* which would be enough to save from oblivion the name of Boissard de Boisdenier; one of the finest Delacroix, *The Judgment of Trajan*, a considerable collection of pictures and sketches by Géri-

Hôtel Bourgtheroulde.
A Coat of Arms.

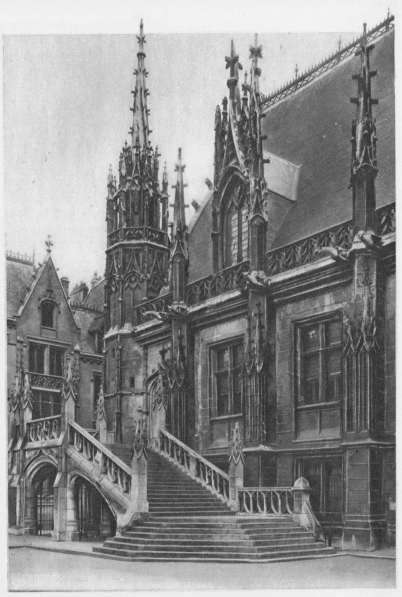

Stairway of the Palais de Justice.

cault, the great Romantic painter of Rouen, and lastly, a fine collection of the impressionists, who often sought in the Norman countryside and its shores the secret of their luminous harmonies. Such a museum alone would justly be the pride of many cities; and in it one can rest, study and meditate.

The Rouen Museum. La Belle Zélie by Ingres.

Beside its civil architecture, rich and attractive as it is, the religious architecture of Rouen is of almost overwhelming grandeur. No more beautiful cathedral exists than that of Notre-Dame, in which one can follow the full development of the evolution of Gothic architecture from the Romanesque period to the full bloom of the flamboyant, on that façade which has recently given Claude Monet the pretext for such a prodigious series of pictures. The Tour de St. Romain unites all three styles with a majestic sobriety equal to that of Chartres. The Tour de Beurre is the most exquisite thing imaginable, with its lace-work and filigree of stone decorating the mighty, aspiring mass. The modern spire of the central tower, like that of Bayeux, has been justly criticised. Seven hundred and forty tons of cast iron do not prevent it from being rather meagre, but it is as ingenious as a contemporary creation can be, which tries to complete the works of an incomparable age. The interior is an accumulation of beauties, from the great front lighted by its rose-window to the stained glass of the transept, the tombs of the Cardinals d'Amboise and of the Brézé family, and the relics of Duke William Longsword and Richard of the Lion Heart. Less majestic, but perhaps of a more intimate charm, are the two churches which form, with Notre-Dame, a splendid trinity of religious art : Saint-Maclou and Saint-Ouen. Saint-Maclou, with its five-arched porch and its doors by Jean Goujon, its stained-glass windows, its cloister with curious galleries of stone and wood; Saint-Ouen, whose modern façade spoils the general effect of the Norman Gothic, which is still splendid in spite of it. And both these sanctuaries are enshrined in a characteristic setting of old wooden houses. If an artist with the cult of the past desires to forget mechanical progress, only a few hours from Paris, and retire into his dreams of vanished centuries, he will find in the neighbourhood of Saint-Maclou and Saint-Ouen plentiful food for his love of silence and his dreaming meditations. But old houses abound on every side in Rouen, where " Old Rouen " has remained a living reality in the whole city, and not only in the Museum of Ceramics, where shine the incomparable collections of old Rouen pottery. This can be seen, among other places, in the Place de La Haute Vieille Tour, the characteristic Rue Eau de Robec and the amazing Rue de l'Epicerie,

Rouen Museum. Sketch by Géricault.

where, above the xvth century gables, one has such a noble vision of the giant towers of the cathedral. The present has been grafted on to these remains of the past without any abrupt transition. The ceaseless and animated life of the industrial port, which is both a sea and a river port, overhung by a cable bridge — the view of the Seine, which broadens out here and is traversed by numerous tugs with their trains of barges; all seems, as it were, to be controlled by the pride and reason of the bronze figure erect upon the point of the Ile Lacroix — that of Pierre Corneille of Rouen who, as Albert Sorel has justly said, was the greatest of the Normans and one of the greatest geniuses of France.

Rouen. The " Tour de Beurre ".

The noble city where Joan of Arc died and Corneille was born, was also the home of Gustave Flaubert. It gave birth to Géricault and counted among its children the actress Champmeslé, the painter Jouvenet, the architect Blondel, the botanist Guy de la Brosse, the moralist Pouchet, the polemist Armand Carrel, Cavalier de la Salle, who won Louisiana for France, Fontenelle, and many other thinkers and men of talent and action. Rouen is one of those places which Barrès has called " centres of psychotherapy ", in which the mind is strengthened and the soul exalted. Here one can learn the lessons of the past, and turn them to use in life. Here is the soul of

Normandy, and no cther city in the land has a more definitely aristocratic and religious spirit — the spirit of a queen among cities, joined to a happy vitality and love of action, which, after ten centuries, are still the qualities of a maritime, commercial and conquering race, reminding us, in spite of many external differences, of the genius of Venice.

Rouen flourishes amidst splendid natural surroundings, at the point where the winding Seine begins to broaden out towards the vast estuary, where the river flows among sand-banks to mingle with the sea. And there, facing out to sea, at the foot of the cliffs of Saint-Adresse

Façade of the Cathedral.

and La Hève, lie the harbours and quays of Le Havre, the second port of France. The site was reclaimed from the salt marshes; and to Francis I belongs all the honour of creating it, and of persisting perseveringly in his intention, in the teeth of the most discouraging beginnings and the spite of nature. It was this king who had the good sense to realise that the river ports of Caudebec, Harfleur and Lillebonne, which were gradually silting up, were no longer sufficient for this estuary, which was one of the keys to his kingdom. In founding the city, which he christened Le Havre de Grâce, he desired to create at once a refuge from storms, a commercial centre and a point of departure for

Flower Market opposite the Cathedral.

great enterprises of exploration or war. The work was carried on, and the city was beginning to take shape, when, one winter, a terribly high tide swept away the houses, sank the ships and swallowed up a number of the inhabitants Once more they set courageously to work. Then came the disaster of the famous galley *La Grande Françoise*, of two

Rouen Cathedral. Tombs of the Cardinals of Amboise.

thousand tons' burden — a Leviathan at that period — which had been built on the spot, but was dashed to pieces against the quay by a storm before it could be launched. Later on, the king resolved to attempt a great naval expedition against England. It was doomed to failure, like all the others which were planned throughout the ages, that of William the Bastard alone succeeding. It was at Le Havre, his own favourite creation, that the king fitted out his squadron; but during the fête at which the great announcement was to be made, the flag-ship caught fire, and was completely burnt in the harbour. In spite of several attempts, the fleet could never reach the shores of England. But royal protection never failed Le Havre. The Protestants summoned the English troops, who installed themselves there till they were turned out by the royal army under Montmorency. Henry IV, Richelieu, Colbert, Louis XVI, the First and Second Empires, never ceased to strengthen the place and enlarge its port. The period of the Great War, during which the Belgian Government and great English camps were established at Le Havre, saw the height of the prosperity of this vast collection of docks, factories and quays, from which liners start for all the countries of the globe.

This is all one can look for at Le Havre, where the pilgrim of art can glean but little, and the past has left scarce a trace; save for the Church of Notre-Dame — which dates from the xviith century, and bears witness to the degeneration of the Renaissance style — and the Arsenal, in the style of Louis XIV,

The Church of Saint-Maclou.

Christ by Clodion.

situated in a picturesque quarter full of old fishermen's houses. One is satisfied to pass delightful moments musing on the great quay, observing its animated crowd and the aviaries of the dealers in birds, or looking on from the old jetty at the manœuvres accompanying the entrance or departure of the gigantic steamers when the sea is rough, as it often is. And yet there is a very good museum at Le Havre, in a rather poor building. Works of some importance are to be found in it, by painters such

Rouen. An old street.

as Roll, Pointelin, Forain, Rafaelli, Courbet, Troyon, Géricault, side by side with old masters, sometimes of doubtful attribution, one of which, signed by Van Dyck, is at least very fine. There are also two works of Pissarro, who often painted at Rouen and Le Havre, and three Claude Monets of the highest order. Lastly, and above all, one can here obtain a complete impression of the high qualities of Eugène Boudin, landscape, animal and marine painter, who was born at Honfleur. He was the son of a small book-seller, who survived him, and presented nearly two hundred and fifty of his studies to Le Havre. Though Eugène Boudin had gained some measure of fame before his death, in spite of his simplicity and modesty, it is only recently that criticism has made a decisive pronouncement as to the real mastery of this skilful and delightful selftaught colourist, who was the direct precursor of impre sionism, and the Corot of these Norman landscapes, to whose rich meadows, marine horizons, estuaries and little ports, with their lovely sailing-boats, he has given such admirable expression, crowning them with skies worthy of the Dutch masters — those Norman skies with their ever-moving procession of clouds, so delicately subtle in their range of blues and grays. Boudin's skies are a revelation of the spirit of Normandy, that tender, moist atmosphere which he has expressed better than anybody. It was Boudin who met the young

Statue of Corneille.

The Church of Saint-Maclou.

Claude Monet at Le Havre and initiated him into the painting of atmosphere, taking him to work with him on the cliffs of Saint-Adresse. Though the pupil has far surpassed his master in fame and power, he has never ceased to do homage to him, and insists on his being ranked high by lovers of art. The works of Boudin, whose production was enormous, figure in many French and foreign collections; but the general effect of the museum at Le Havre remains unrivalled. It is the only note of art in the birthplace of the Scudérys, Casimir Delavigne and Bernardin de Saint-Pierre.

Above all, Le Havre owes its fame to its port and to its commercial activity. Each year shows a sensible growth of the harbour. In 1923 it already dealt with a traffic of 4,500,000 tons and the continual improvements lead one to expect an ever increasing development.

Moreover, the tonnage recorded takes no account of sporadic traffic or of the ships of considerable size which ply between the port and Rouen.

Le Havre is one of the most important export centres for goods destined for America; for France it is the central market for

Channel steamers in the harbour at Havre.

leather, wool, cotton and coffee. It is an excellent centre for the tourist who wishes to travel through Normandy and to visit the Valley of the Seine. The river may be seen in all its calm majesty. Even though it has

A Seascape by Boudin (Havre Museum).

not the turbulence of the Rhone nor the grandeur of the Loire, it yet possesses an intimate character entirely its own. The green river banks are charming and peaceful; the innumerable windings of the river give an added charm to the tourist and one feels that the country is a vigo-rous and happy one. And when the tide in flood meets the still ebbing waters running sea-ward, the swirl-ing eddy of foam presents a rare spec-tacle.

Opposite Le Havre, on the left bank of the estuary, rises the most

A Still Life by Boudin (Havre Museum).

charming and typical port of old Normandy; and here the pilgrim of art may rejoice that nature, by invading the shore with mud, and so depriving it of a beach, has saved delightful Honfleur from being spoilt and vulgarised as a seaside resort. Tourists go there by thousands, all the same, but they do not stay there, and its character is left untouched. One could hardly imagine a prettier little seaport, which might have been created for the joy of painters. It is very ancient, and has had its own fine, brave series of historic events. The English naturally attacked it on several occasions. Their king Edward III took possession of it. When they returned at the end of the xivth century, they were driven off, but at the beginning of the xvth century, a daring English raid carried off a whole fleet of ships from Honfleur. But the sailors of Honfleur, in rivalry with those of St. Malo and Dieppe, were a great anxiety to the hereditary enemy; and it was in this little port that was organised, in the middle of the xvth century, an expedition for harrying the British shores. From here famous explorers set forth; among them Paulmier de Gonneville, who touched at an island supposed to be the great southern continent, Denis, who touched at Brazil and discovered Newfoundland for France, and the most famous of all, Samuel de Champlain, the coloniser of Canada. It was not till the loss of Newfoundland and Canada, the silting up of its harbour, and the rise of Le Havre on the opposite shore, that the prestige of Honfleur began to fade. It had to give up all great enterprises and confine itself to coastwise trade; but it is still a very lively, active port, full of sailing-boats, whose tangle of masts and rigging is one of its attractions.

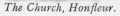

The Church, Honfleur.

The artist will find at Honfleur the amazing church of St. Catherine. It was built by the shipbuilders at the end of the xvth century, and they made it entirely of wood, save for the foundations. They carved it in the flamboyant style and decked it with loving care, like those votive frigates which the pious and ingenious mariners of yore used to enclose in bottles or hang up in chapels. This is the sole instance in the history of Norman art of a church tower separate from its church, like the campanili standing

Honfleur. Notre-Dame de Grâce.

by Italian sanctuaries. It stands on a little *place*, and its ancient woodwork is shored up by slate-covered supports. The Lieutenance standing by it is equally charming, with its carved beams, its brown tiled roofs mellowed by time, its corner turrets and its appealing atmosphere of antiquity. How many a painter has enthusiastically set up his easel there ! And what a joy it must have been to them to make sketches of the Old Harbour, with its row of xviiith century houses, with carved corbels crowded with amusing details, and closely covered with a scalework of slate, like the chain-mail hauberks of William's knights, which on sunny or on grey days alike take on exquisite tones of ashen or bluish grey. Nowhere could one find a better example of the persistent survival of the life of these little Norman ports of bygone days, throwing down, as it were, a challenge to modern ideas. But one understands its spirit even better if one pays a visit to the museum of Old Honfleur. It is partly arranged in the nave of the secularised church of St. Etienne, so curious with its wooden porch and belfry, and in the neighbouring xvith century houses, which are also of wood. A series of interiors characteristic of Caux and Honfleur have been carefully and intelligently

Honfleur. The Museum.

arranged, to represent the home life of the middle classes, the peasants, the fisherman, sailors, pirates, and even the captains of slave-ships. Beside this museum, with its reconstitution of the past, the one containing contemporary paintings naturally pales; but all the same it contains a few canvasses of Boudin and Ribot and of less famous painters such as Nozal, Tattegrain or Renouf, who was a good painter of the maritime life of Normandy. At Honfleur were born Paulmier de Gonneville, Admiral Hamelin, the economist Le Play, Eugene Boudin, the great historian Albert Sorel, and that curious and charming humorist Alphonse Allais, to whom must be added the novelist-poetess Mᵐᵉ Lucie Delarue-Mardrus, with her fanatical devotion to Honfleur and Normandy, and the famous poet and prose-writer Henri de Régnier.

Honfleur adds to all these attractions those of a flourishing countryside, the most celebrated point of which — and justly so — is the hill of the Côte de Grâce, with its pilgrimage of Our Lady, from which one is never tired of gazing upon Le Havre, the beginning of the estuary up to Tancarville and the vast expanse of the sea. And so the course of the Seine, which, from the Ile-de-France onwards, has never ceased to deligth the traveller, comes to a triumphal end.

Honfleur. The Governor's House.

Lisieux. The Cathedral from the Public Gardens.

CHAPTER V

—

Evreux — Lisieux — Pont-l'Evêque, the district of Auge — Seaside places from Honfleur to the Orne.

If we make our way from the Ile-de-France into Normandy, leaving the valley of the Seine at Mantes and turning aside towards Orne and Calvados, in the direction of Caen, Evreux is the first important town which marks on this side the imaginary frontier of the Norman land. Evreux appears, looking charming in the background, surrounded by green hills and lying stretched out along the three branches of the Itou. It is a very old Gallo-Roman city, which became a diocese and a countship after passing through terrible trials. The wretched city was stormed, sacked and burnt by the Northmen, the Count of Paris, the Count of Blois, the Danes, the English, John Lackland and the King of France, one after the other. It also lived through some tragic hours under the Revolution, when it took sides with the Girondins, whose hopes of a federalist rising were dashed by the battle at Vernon. Nowadays Evreux is an elegant and peaceful provincial town, proud of its fine buildings; among which are its cathedral of Notre-Dame, a Romanesque church, rebuilt in the Norman Gothic style, and transformed in the course of centuries by all the graces of the Gothic and flamboyant styles, a little incongruously, perhaps, but none the less with a noble charm. The same term applies to the old flamboyant episcopal palace, now a lycée, the pretty Tour de l'Horloge, the abbey of Saint-Taurin (the first bishop of Evreux), masked in the xviith century by an undistinguished

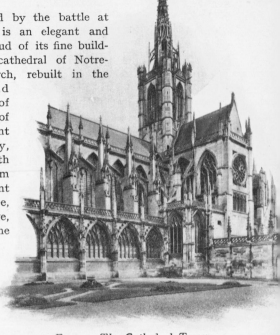

Evreux. The Cathedral Tower.

façade, behind which one discovers a pure alliance of the Romanesque and Gothic styles. Evreux is surrounded by a fresh, soft type of country, in which lies Le Neubourg, with its ruined castles and its bloody memories of the past, and the remains of the abbey of Bec-Hellouin, a thousand years old, which was so famous under the famous theologians, Lanfranc and St. Anselm, who came from Italy, and became priors of it in succession before becoming in turn Archbishops of Canterbury, after the Norman Conquest of England.

And so we come to Conches, which is quite a little town on a steep eminence. Small as it is, it has

Evreux. A Doorway in the Clock Tower.

also had the misfortune to be coveted by the great, and has fallen victim to their quarrels. having been taken and sacked in turn by Philip-Augustus, the Duke of Lancaster. Dugues-clin and the armies of the League. At Conches we are quite in Normandy, in that smiling land where the fighting was so fierce during the intermin-able duel between the kings of France and the English, bent upon keeping their ancestral duchy — a duel lasting six hundred years and as bitter as the one of which the territories of Lorraine were the object, in the struggle between the Latin and Germanic races. Tra-vellers enjoying their holidays, who traverse this region in order to reach the seaside, have no idea of all these burnings, massacres and exactions; but the tale is told by the buildings. Humanity paid very dearly in Normandy for its fi-

Evreux. The Cathedral Tower.

delity to the crown of France during the Hundred Years' War, and later for its sympathy with Calvinism during the wars of religion. The traces of Philip Augustus, Edward and Henry of England, and Henry IV are visible on every side, and properties have constantly passed from hand to hand. Beaumont-le-Roger raises its church of St. Nicolas against the background of a fine forest, and the imposing ruins of its priory of

La Trinité-Bernay were once a fortress sacked by Charles the Bad, by the Huguenots and Leaguers, where, in the dark days of 1870, the National Guards put up a brave defence against the advance of the German divisions. All this neighbourhood is cut by valleys of a brilliant green, dotted with white farm-houses with their exposed brown beams, around which graze countless herds of cattle. It is a stock-breeding region with rich pastures, a peculiarly fruitful and peaceful land, with châteaux here and there, the most famous of which was that of Chamblais, near Bernay, rechristened Broglie in 1716 in honour of the Piedmontese family to whom it was presented, the title of duke and a peerage of France being attached to the property. But there is scarcely a hamlet which does not preserve some untouched trace of the past.

Evreux. The Clock Tower.

And so we come to the valley of the Touques, which, like the parallel valley of the Dives, cuts across the old district of Auge. Here is Lisieux, sombre and ruddy, built of brick and grey stone, enclosed, as in a velvet case, within the curved valley formed by the surrounding range of hills, beneath a sky which is often overcast. As the traveller leaves the station he can see at a glance that here is one of those towns in which the ancient soul of a race or region is left intact.

Lisieux was the Gallic city of the Lexoviani — hence the name of Lexoviens still borne by its inhabitants — and since the early days of

Christianity it has been the seat of a bishop, and councils have been held there. Its earliest trials were inflicted upon it by Geoffrey Plantagenet, who took possession of it after a siege marked by deeds of savage cruelty. It was in the cathedral, the earliest monument of Gothic religious architecture built in Normandy, that Henry II Plantagenet's union with Eleanor of Aquitaine was consecrated, an important event which created the Angevin Empire, stretching from the Pyrenees to England, and placed the Frankish monarchy in mortal peril.

Beaumont-le-Roger. A Street.

When Philip Augustus undertook to break its power, his determined campaign for seizing Normandy and making it French involved the recapture of Lisieux. It also suffered during the Hundred Years' War; and, much later, the Leaguers and Protestants fought for its possession. It would be impossible to find a more typically Norman atmosphere than in this venerable little city, in which some noble buildings are to be found within a limited space. First, the cathedral of St. Pierre, rebuilt on the site of the original Romanesque church in the XIIth century, with its two unequal towers, its central tower, the fine austerity of its interior, and the exquisite mel-

Beaumont-le-Roger. A Street.

In Lisieux.

lowness of its weathered stonework. Here lay beneath its pavement the remains of Joan of Arc's base judge, Pierre Cauchon, formerly Bishop of Beauvais, who was driven out by his flock for selling himself to the English and Burgundians, and died as Bishop of Lisieux. On the site of his tomb pious hands have recently set up a statue of the heroine of whose condemnation he was the cause. The church of St. Jacques is less imposing, but is a delightful example of the flamboyant style. But the artistic and archaelogical interest of Lisieux lies in the state of preservation of its many old houses, which revive visions of the past on every side. The Rue aux Fèvres is particularly celebrated. From one end to the other, it presents a line of carved façades, in the Gothic or Renaissance styles — to the latter of which belongs the Manoir de la Salamandre, near a xvith century bridge and washing-places. The general effect is a joy to etchers and may be compared to the famous Rue Eau de Robec at Rouen. The Rue au Char, the Grande Rue, the Rue d'Ouville have also some of these fine houses of carved wood and slate scale-work, and the interior of the old episcopal palace — now the Law Courts — contains some very rich decoration.

Lisieux has recently acquired fresh prestige from the fact of having

Lisieux. The Cathedral Square.

given birth to the young Carmelite nun canonised under the name of Saint Theresa of the Child Jesus, known to the tender devotion of thousands of the faithful as " little Sister Theresa of Lisieux ". The valleys surrounding the town are fruitfulness itself, and it is a joy to wander about all the valley of the Touques, which bounds the district of Auge,

Lisieux. St. Jacques.

towards Norolles or Orbec, where we come upon châteaux in the grand style, like that of Fervacques, with its huge elms, or that of Mailloc with its warlike appearance and crenellated towers, full of fine works of art, pictures by Fragonard, Bassano and Ruysdael, with portraits and relics of the famous Laplace, who lived in this family property. We must go on nearly as far as Vimoutiers to visit the farm of Le Ronceray, where Charlotte Corday was born, or the church of the hamlet of Ecorches where she was baptised. Mézidon offers nothing of interest, but gourmets may well be allowed a brief space to salute the villages called Camembert and Livarot. Throughout this whole region of Lisieux, cheese forms one of the glories, as well as earning the profits of the land of Normandy. It also gives its reputation to Pont-l'Evêque, which we shall find in the heart of the district of Auge, situated between a line running from Lisieux to Mézidon and one running from Dives to Pont-l'Evêque, including the two parallel valleys of the Dives and the Touques. It is a land of plenty, a great orchard full of apple-trees yielding an incomparable cider, which forms a traditional element in the fame of Normandy. Cheese and cider are the source of the wealth of the district of Auge. Pont-l'Evêque is a very quiet, old-fashioned, gay little city, rising from velvety meadows, with some old houses, a church of St. Michael, in the flamboyant style, with stained glass which many a cathedral might envy; and the " Pont-episcopiens ", as its inhabitants are called, are certainly not to be pitied. Indeed, nobody seems in need of pity in this wealthy region of good cheer and good

Lisieux. Old Houses.

humour, full of delightful little country towns, such as Saint-André-d'Hébertot, and good inns in which the living is such as to banish all gloom.

Eastwards, in the direction of the Seine, the district of Auge extends as far as

A Farm in Auge.

Pont-Audemer, on the Risle, another of those tiny old cities where there is not much to see, but which charm us by their kindly atmosphere and fine situation. Since the VIIIth century, when a certain lord named Audemer, or Omer, built a bridge there, beside which the houses grouped themselves, the people of Pont-Audemer have had no history; and the charter granted to the commune by Philip Augustus seems to have protected them. Obscure but happy, they have been glad to dispense with the honour of being attacked, pillaged or burnt by the English or the Leaguers, or figuring in the secular duel of the Hundred Years' War or the struggles between Catholics and Huguenots. They have enjoyed peace, which is worth more than anything else; and they have their pretty church of Saint-Ouen, some amusing, tumble-down houses, and a little harbour full of sandbanks which sends boatloads of cider-apples to England. To the north of Pont-Audemer, almost touching the Seine, the lover of scenery will do well to push on as far as that astonishing cliff of La Roque, more than a hundred yards high, which descends abruptly at the point where the Risle falls into the estuary of the Seine; or to the strange region called the " Marsh of Vernier ", near Quillebœuf. This marsh, created by the filling up of a creek on the left bank of the

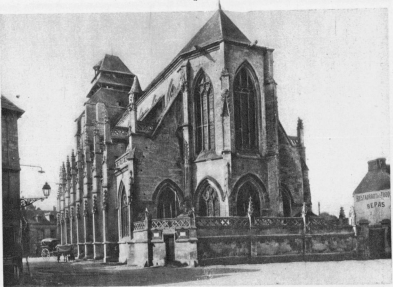

Pont-l'Evêque. The Church.

Pont-l'Evêque. The Banks of the Touque.

Seine with soil washed down by the river, is cut by embankments and canals, and divided into cottage-gardens, cultivated zones and treacherous quicksands. By its wild melancholy, its damp atmosphere, its stretches of reeds and its vast silences, it recalls that Brière region near Nantes which has been made famous by Alphonse de Chateaubriand's fine novel.

All this attractive district of Auge, between Honfleur and the Orne, leads up to a coast whose watering-places are famous. This reputation is certainly due far less to the attractiveness of the places themselves than to their proximity to Paris and to the whims of fashion. In fact, the scenery is lacking in character. It is flat and ordinary in comparison with the beauties of Fécamp, Etretat, Honfleur, Saint-Vaast, La Hague, Granville, or Mont Saint-Michel. From the splendid Côte de Grâce to Trouville, by way of Cricquebœuf and Villerville, the great cliffs grow gradually smaller and smaller. Villerville is still picturesque, but at Trouville begin the low dunes and sandy beaches which stretch in monotonous insignificance as far as Port en Bessin. On the two banks of the mouth of the Orne, this sandy curve presents the same appearance; and we may ask ourselves why, when their merit, or lack of merit, is equal, the western bank is given over to a clientèle with moderate incomes, content with poor hotels, or existing cheaply in furnished apartments,

Criquebœuf. The Church.

without modern comforts or easy communications; while the eastern bank is a centre of luxury and of every refinement of comfort which progress can devise. Nature is no more beautiful at Trouville or Deauville than at Langrune or Arromanches. Trouville, indeed, preserves to a certain extent its character as a little old port at the mouth of the muddy Touques. One can see properly-rigged boats there, and its fishermen are not a myth. It has some trade and is connected with Le Havre by steamer. Here we find installed, as best they can manage, a crowd of sea-bathers of all sorts, from the millionaires in their sumptuous villas to the modest guests at the popular restaurants and inns, and the excursionists. It is hard to understand why this crowd hailed Trouville as a queen of watering-places, until the recent development of Deauville dethroned this supremacy, so tolerant of the diversions of the populace. It was the fashionable society of the Second Empire that created Deauville, which will doubtless remain in history as the most remarkable achievement of the duc de Morny. A great battle between conflicting interests was fought out by journalists and financiers on the banks of the Touques, even more desperate than those of the English and Normans in the Middle Ages. It was Deauville which won. A city was built by the might of gold, so opulent and rich in pleasures that amid the attractions of the casino, the theatre, the enormous palace hotels, the tables, the races, the procession of Parisian celebrities, — both in society and the demi-monde, — about as much interest is taken in the sea as at Monte-Carlo. It would be absolutely useless, and even out of place, did it not serve as a pretext for dressing up. The plutocracy of Deauville does not tolerate that mixture of classes which, at Trouville, permits some contact between slender purses and great fortunes. Deauville, with its display of unbridled luxury, boasts of being the greatest " Potinière ", or centre of gossip, in France. But all this has nothing to do with Normandy, and that interest in art, nature and history which are the motive of this book.

The surroundings of Trouville-Deauville, those rival sisters which the narrow channel of the Touques is wide enough to separate, are not very interesting; and it is not hard to find anywhere in Normandy something better than the Forest of Saint-Gatien or the view from the " Mont " Camisy, with its altitude of 330 feet. Bénerville and Blonville are quieter neighbouring watering-places, where those visitors stay who find it interesting to go and look on at the high life of Deauville without having to face the ruinous charges of its hotels. Villers and Houlgate, the next two places, are refined and aristocratic summer resorts, among rather more interesting scenery. The château of Villers is fine, and picturesque nature once more takes her right place during the walk to the lofty, sombre cliffs known as the Vaches Noires, above which lies that strange jumble of rocks called, not too inappropriately, the Désert du Chaos, which gives its character to Houlgate. The old

Dives. Memorial Column to William the Conqueror.

town of Dives, at the mouth of the Dives, was a port in the Middle Ages. But it is now silted up, and the sea has withdrawn to a distance of over a mile. Dives has only one thing to recall in its humble history, but that is a thing of importance; for it was here that in 1066 William the Bastard assembled the great fleet with which he was to set out and conquer England. The winds, however, were contrary, and the bulk of his ships set out from Saint-Valéry. English visitors never fail to visit the neighbouring hill, bearing the name of Arcisse de Caumont, the great archaeologist of Bayeux, who set up a column on it to commemorate the event. They also go and read the names of the barons who set sail with William, carved above the doorway of the pretty flamboyant church of Dives. But it is not given to all to go into the Hôtellerie de Guillaume le Conquérant, or to stay there. It is a charming old dwelling-house transformed into a museum of Norman art by a proprietor of taste, who knows how to distinguish visitors with a true taste for art, and reserves his favour for them. Lastly, Cabourg, a pleasant but quite modern watering-place, is the last before the neighbourhood of Varaville, Le Home and the pastures and sand-dunes which mark the estuary of the Orne, opposite Ouistreham and Caen.

Dives. Escutcheon of the Hôtellerie de Guillaume.

The Caen Canal.

CHAPTER VI

—

Caen, Bayeux, and the Seaside Resorts
from the Orne to Cherbourg.

Caen is, with Rouen, the most important city in Normandy, and vies with it in the number and beauty of its antiquities. Its surroundings are inferior, but it claims to surpass Rouen by virtue of an intellectual activity, both past and present, of which it is justly proud. It maintains this reputation by means of its Academy, its learned societies, and its University. If Rouen was the favourite city of Rollo, Caen was that of his descendant, William the Conqueror. In the ancient city of Catumagos, Latinised into Cadomus, the duke set up his residence. He fortified it, built himself a castle and, in pious concert with Queen Matilda, built there the two Abbeys of St. Etienne, or the Abbaye aux Hommes, and, La Trinité, or the Abbaye aux Dames, in order to expiate their marriage within the prohibited degrees, which took place without the permission of the Pope. When it returned to the hands of the Kings of France, Caen became rich and flourishing. But it was to undergo heavy trials. It was taken by storm and sacked by Edward III of England. Seventy years later it suffered the same fate at the hands of Henry V, who held it and

Caen. Apse of Saint-Pierre.

beautified it. It was the Regent Bedford who founded its University. An attempt of thirty thousand peasants to free it from the English yoke met with a bloody reverse, and Caen had to wait till the victory of Formigny drove the English from Norman soil once for all. The city had yet to suffer pillage and assault on various occasions at the hands of the Calvinists, besides two terrible plagues, the disorders of the Fronde, and finally of the Revolution. It enthusiastically welcomed the Girondins and the federal ideal which they opposed to Jacobin centralisation. The defeat of the federalists at Vernon ruined the hopes of the Girondins; but it was from Caen that Charlotte Corday set out, revolted by the crimes of the Terror, and determined to kill Marat. Since then the city has enjoyed peace and a prosperity due at first to stock-breeding, agriculture, trade, and the transport of goods down the Orne to Ouistreham and the sea, but recently increased tenfold by the revival of the iron-mines in this neighbourhood.

These mines had been worked during the Middle Ages, but afterwards abandoned. The methodical plans of the Germans for an industrial invasion had led them to acquire a large majority of the concessions for these mines in Calvados; but the war ousted them, and led to an enormous revival in the working of this subterranean wealth. A vast work of organisation is being carried out on the banks of the Orne, a great industrial city is growing up beside the old town, and Caen is destined to become a great centre of metallurgy and a considerable river-port whose tonnage is bound to increase. Its natural position, the resources of the soil and of what lies beneath it, are a guarantee of this. But it will jealously endeavour to maintain its intellectual position; and modern progress leaves its living past untouched. The factories, railways, canals, and great blast-furnaces are a thing apart from old Caen with its abbeys, — the noble city of churches, the birthplace of Malherbe, full of old, picturesque houses, some of which, in exquisitely wrought stone or wood, are as fine as the most celebrated houses in Rouen.

Caen. Hôtel d'Escoville.

There are many of them to be found even in the Rue St. Jean, which is its most animated street. It leads past the old church of St. Jean, which is built in a fine flamboyant style, but is unfinished, and has been cracked by the subsidence of its foundations in the marshy ground — to the principal *place*, where the Cathedral of St. Pierre, a gem lovingly carved by successive generations for four centuries, raises to a height of 260 feet its famous spire, a marvel of elegance, and the classic type of all the church towers born of Norman art. Almost opposite St. Pierre one finds, somewhat hidden, two masterpieces of the Renaissance, the Hotel de Than and the Hotel d'Escoville. The former of these is still partly

Abbaye aux Dames.

shut in by sordid old houses, and the blackened old façade of the second would hardly lead one to suspect the exquisite perfection of its inner courtyard, with its staircase crowned by openwork lanterns, its statues of David and Judith, and its reliefs representing the rescue of Andromeda and the rape of Europa. Nowhere will the artist who loves the French architecture of the xvith century find anything more pure and exquisite. The Hotel de Than has dormer windows as elegant as those of Anet, Azay or Chenonceaux. But at Caen we have too often cause to regret that these gems are not properly shown off or protected from damage. It is a town where one has often to take some trouble to look for the fine remains of the past, hidden away in old and evil-smelling streets. But in the Rue St. Pierre, at any rate, can easily be seen some precious houses with statuettes and carved beams, crowned by amusing gables. The church in the Rue Froide, once known as Notre-Dame de Froide Rue, is also a rare and very fine building, with its noble combination of the Gothic and Renaissance styles, due, like the Cathedral of St. Pierre, to the genius of Hector Sohier, one of the most amazing architects of the xvith century.

And so we come to the Abbaye aux Hommes, an imposing sight, though the neighbouring houses, and the adjacent buildings of the Lycée Malherbe, prevent one from falling back to a sufficient distance to grasp the com-

Abbaye aux Hommes. Choir Screen.

Caen. Abbaye aux Hommes.

plete effect of this Romanesque-Gothic mass, rebuilt and modified throughout a period of four hundred years, with its two pointed towers 295 feet high, its tiered roof, its pinnacles, and the massive buttresses which once upheld a central tower 390 feet high. It was beneath these grand, austere arches that the founder, William the Conqueror, was buried, ten years after the consecration of the abbey. Here, too, took place one of the strangest and most famous scenes in the Middle Ages, often retold, but never so admirably as by Augustin Thierry. It is he who has best expressed all the pathos of the hue and cry *(" clameur de haro ")* raised during the funeral service by the plebeian Asselin, who proclaimed before everybody that the site of the church had been that of his father's house, seized by the dead man and never paid for. Upon

Caen. Hôtel de Than.

this the ceremony was broken off, and an immediate enquiry was made; and when the man's emphatic allegations were proved to be true, the bishops and barons clubbed together to pay him his due. This pathetic episode was succeeded by a scene of horror. When the service was finished, they began to lower the great heavy coffin of the corpulent William into the tomb which awaited it. The tomb was too narrow, and they tried to force it in to make an end of it; upon which the coffin burst, and such a terrible stench arose from the decaying body, that the priests, not daring to flee, but suffocated — as was indeed the

Caen. Doorway of the Abbaye aux Hommes.

whole congregation — rushed through the last rites, and left alone in this foul atmosphere the high and mighty Duke of Normandy and King of England. In later days the tomb was violated by the Protestants in the xvith century, and the Revolution caused the remains of William to be scattered to the winds.

At the side of the Church of St. Etienne rises the Lycée Malherbe, housed in the old abbey, which was rebuilt in the xviiith century, and definitively converted to this use in 1804. It is certainly the finest lycée in France, and is unique of its sort; a palatial lycée in which one finds a profusion of fine panelling, some pictures by Le Brun and Lépicié, a staircase which is a masterpiece of architecture and ironwork, a cloister and a refectory whose stone facings would make the fortune of many an antiquarian. The girls' Normal School forms part of this great group of buildings, housed in a well-restored building of the xiiith century; and not far away is the old Romanesque church of St. Nicholas, used as a store-house for forage, like the church of the Vieux Sauveur, which is now a corn market. Caen can indulge in this melancholy luxury, for it has too many churches. There is the church of Vieux St. Etienne, an Anglo-Norman building with a noble porch and a fine tower. The town possesses Saint-Ouen, Notre-Dame de la Gloriette, the Saint-Sépulcre, converted into a shop, Saint-Gilles, which is falling into ruins, and others

Château de Fontaine-Henry.

besides. It has its fascinating *Musée des Antiquaires Normands,* so precious for the study of the local legends of the saints. Finally, it has the church of La Trinité, or the Abbaye aux Dames, founded by Queen Matilda, whose daughter was the first abbess. The queen and Anne de Montmorency sleep beneath the choir of this edifice, which, though less enormous than the Abbaye aux Hommes, is no less majestic, with its soft harmonious Romanesque style and its fine towers. The castle in some sort commands the city. Its xɪth century keep was razed at the Revolution, but its ramparts and bastions, adorned with clumps of trees, have made of it a pleasant and picturesque spot. Lastly, the Town Hall contains a very considerable library and a remarkably well arranged picture-gallery, in which are to be found works of fine quality : a magnificent Perugino, several pictures by Veronese, a Cima, a Tiepolo, a Tintoretto, a Carpaccio, some Dutch masters, and, among the moderns, Courbet, Lépine, Daubigny, Tassaert, and a canvas as fine as a Corot by an almost unknown Norman landscape painter, named Rame.

Caen possesses all those elements which go to make up the charm of a city : it has a very busy harbour, a number of buildings of the highest order, a University, learned societies of recognised merit, seaside resorts close at hand, exquisite beauty spots on the banks of the Orne, and a

race-course from which the view, embracing the whole city which its
spires and towers, is as attractive as anyone could wish. None the less,
it is a dusty, dismal town, and is not very pleasing to the visitor's eye.
The country round is fertile, but flat and lacking in character, unless one
follows the course of the Orne as far up as Clécy. The plain of Caen, swept
by winds from both sea and land, is like the Beauce in little, treeless, and
gradually becoming depopulated since the war; and its villages are quite
uninteresting. There are, however, a few châteaux worthy of note scattered about, for instance in the west, the château of Lasson or Fontaine-
Henri, two sumptuous dwelling-houses of the Renaissance, or that of
Thierry-Harcourt towards the south.

Bayeux, the old capital of the Gauls in the Bessin, where Saint-
Exupère founded a bishopric as early as 360, was one of the first cities
to be occupied by the Northmen. It, too, has passed through vicissitudes
and endured sieges. But for centuries past, nothing has troubled the
calm lethargy of this charming little city, where the grass grows between
the cobble-stones. Except for one or two streets, which are full of life on
market days, all is silence —- but a silence which is pleasant and tranquil,
rather than sad. It is good to ramble about these deserted streets, where
one's attention is arrested from time to time by an old dwelling house of

Château de Lasson.

Bayeux. Gateway.

the xvth or xviith century, side by side with some ancient carved wooden house; and where one catches a glimpse, through some half-open doorway at the end of an ancient garden, of the pure façade of a gentleman's house, in which many a secluded life has dreamed itself away. Bayeux drowses in the shadow of its Cathedral of Notre-Dame, one of the finest in Normandy, and indeed in the whole of France. It would be impossible to find a more complete example of the Gothic art of Normandy. In this huge building there scarcely remain any traces of the original Romanesque basilica, which it replaced in the early years of the xiith century. The two towers, 250 feet high, are the definitive type of all those silhouettes which point skywards, from the Cotentin to the district of Caux. The xvth century central tower, in the flamboyant style, was crowned in the xvith century with an ugly dome; seventy years ago this threatened to collapse, and a bronze spire was constructed in the flamboyant style, which suits it better. The interior is full of fine detail, and the exterior, which is seen to advantage from a spacious *place*, is imposing in its calm majesty. Rising on Romanesque foundations, the Gothic genius soars upwards with a spirit and dignity which are both beautiful and moving. The other attraction of Bayeux is the famous Tapestry of Queen Matilda, in an enormous glass case in the old episcopal palace, now turned into a Museum. It is not a tapestry at all, but a mere embroidery in different coloured wools on an unbleached linen

Bayeux. Hôtel de Fresne. (Detail).

background, 230 feet long. It was not the Queen who embroidered it, but doubtless some Anglo-Saxon craftsmen, by order of Odo, Bishop of Bayeux, a natural brother of the Conqueror, to whom the Queen presented it with the intention of having it preserved in the cathedral. The work is rather coarse, but its value as a document has made it celebrated throughout the whole world; for by its faithful and naive presentation, it gives us a mass of information upon the manners and customs of the early xıth century. The tapestry sets forth a series of episodes, clumsily but often expressively drawn, the figures in which are intermingled with an embroidered Latin legend. They relate the history of the quarrel between Harold and William, who started by being friends; the bequest of the throne of England to William by Edward the Confessor, Harold's treacherous usurpation, the fury of William, his preparations by land and sea to go and defend his rights

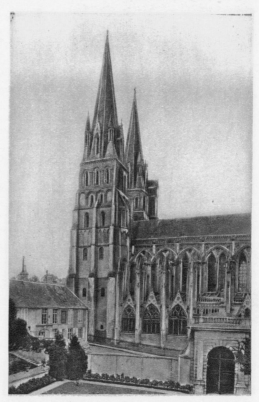

Bayeux. The Cathedral.

beyond the channel, and finally the Battle of Hastings, the victory of the Northmen over the Saxons, and the death of Harold. It can well be imagined that a visit to this tapestry forms a regular pilgrimage for thousands of Britons.

Bayeux is situated in the midst of a verdant countryside; the surrounding country has the flat and somewhat insignificant character of

the plain of Caen, except in the direction of Saint-Lô, and a few interesting châteaux, such as those of Sully, Brécy and Creully, are to be found here

and there. It may be said that all this northern region of Calvados and the Bessin is far the least picturesque in Normandy. It slopes down to a coast without cliffs, in which one may seek in vain for the in-spiriting views of Etretat or the Co-tentin.  Starting from the left bank and estuary of the Orne, Caen has its hinterland of seaside resorts. Near the little port of Ouistreham, to which

the traffic between Caen and Le Havre lends animation, the Orne dis-
solves into sand and grass-lands good for grazing sheep and duck-shooting.

There is nothing
worthy of note
about the watering-
places of Lion, Luc,
Saint-Aubin, Ber-
nières and Courseul-
les, except for a
rather fine church
at Bernières, a nice
little Renaissance
château at Lion,
and inland the pil-
grimage of La Déli-
vrande, where a miraculously exhumed Virgin attracts numbers of the
faithful, and is the annual pretext for a considerable procession. Cour-

— 93 —

seulles is a fishing-port with no great output, on the modest river Seulle. These sandy beaches, backed by low dunes, draw a uniform and worthy clientèle of unpretentious summer visitors to this series of villages with humble casinos and poor provisions. These seaside resorts are treated, as it were, like poor relations by the luxurious and well-equipped watering-places on the other side of the Orne, from Cabourg to Trouville. The same is true of the watering-places of the Bessin forming the hinterland of Bayeux on the north, such as Asnelles, Arromanches or Vierville. Port-en-Bessin alone, thanks to its unusual situation, has the appearance of an old-world fishing-port, still fit to tempt painters. There is nothing distinctive about Formigny, where, in 1450, took place the battle which was to drive the English from Norman soil for good. We have to go as far as Grandcamp to see the end of this dull stretch of coast, and, above all, to Isigny, situated where the Aire and the Vire join the sea, and animated by its sailing boats and its brisk trade in the local butter, the greatest centre of which inland is Carentan near by.

Bayeux. An old House.

Here we are on the threshold of the Cotentin, where the coast takes a sharp bend to the north; where the landscape changes, the cliffs grow

Between Caen and Bayeux. Château de Crevilly.

higher, and nature once more appears in her full grandeur. This eastern coast of the Cotentin, like the western coast, is comparatively little frequented. Fashionable visitors would be bored by it, and people with narrow incomes consider it too far from Paris, owing to the expensive journey. These reasons will for some time to come protect the peninsula form the vulgarity of sea-side life. All the same, one can live very well in the amusing sea-side village of Quinéville, within sight of which rise the three granite islets of Saint-Marcouf. Morsalines is a gem in a setting of verdure on the shore of its harmonious little bay. Saint-Vaast, on its peninsula, has an imposing air with its fortifications planned by Vauban, and its island of Tatihou, which was once fortified; and life there is easy, simple, and far more likely to charm the artist than that of the seaside resorts of Calvados or the Orne. This region is haunted by the heroic and mournful memory of the battle of 1692. In order to restore James II of England to his throne, a great naval expedition had been decided upon, a regular French Armada. D'Estrées was to sail from Brest with his squadron and join Tourville off Cherbourg before making a raid northwards. A storm prevented d'Estrées from reaching the appointed place; and Tourville found himself facing unsupported the English and Dutch

Saint-Vaast. La Hougue.

fleets, which were twice as strong as his own. He had definite orders to give battle at all costs. He obeyed, but was overpowered, in spite of prodigious feats of skill and daring. He managed to effect the escape of part of his ships towards the west by doubling Cape La Hague in the direction of Jersey; but was forced to retreat with the rest into the bay of La Hougue.

Saint-Vaast. La Hougue

Bayeux. The Choir of the Cathedral.

The victorious enemy hemmed him in. Rather than surrender, the great admiral's ships ran aground, and were annihilated by the English fire-ships. For long afterwards the shore was strewn with the débris of this vast disaster. To this sad, but yet glorious memory is added, in these regions, that of the shipwreck of 1120, in which the White Ship was swallowed up on its way to France with all the family of Henry I of England, and the flower of the noble English lords and ladies. This took place off Gatteville and Barfleur, a region as wild as the most famous parts of Brittany, which, again like Brittany, has *menhirs* to show in the interior, like those of Saint Pierre Eglise and Cosqueville. And here we come in sight of the Ile Pelée and the forts of Cherbourg.

Country around Barfleur.

Cherbourg. The Docks.

CHAPTER VII

—

Cherbourg, the Cotentin, Coutances, Avranches

Though there are no buildings worthy of interest to be found at Cherbourg, it is none the less a very old town, one of the cities of the Unelles, a tribe of the Gauls who occupied this region before the coming of the Roman legions. Cherbourg was their chief port. Queen Matilda founded there in the xith century the Abbey of Notre-Dame du Vœu, and later on Philip Augustus realised the importance of the situation of Cherbourg for the defence of the Channel. He turned it into a military port which

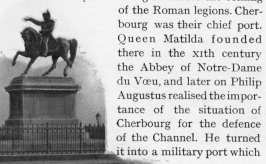

Cherbourg. Statue of Napoleon.

La Hague. The Environs.

the Kings of France were constantly improving. Vauban began immense works for the protection of the roadstead, but the great disaster of La Hougue supervened.

Later, Louis XVI had Vauban's fortifications destroyed, and built some more effective ones. But in the meanwhile, in 1768, the English fleet came and daringly set fire to the ships anchored in the roadstead, landing companies which occupied the unfortified town. It remained for Napoleon, the most illustrious and tenacious enemy of England, to give Cherbourg an armour proof

Cherbourg. A Corner of the Port.

Cherbourg Luggers.

Rocks and Lighthouse at La Hague.

against all attacks. It was he who carried on the construction of the huge artificial mole which forms the roadstead, and a system of forts which really seemed impregnable in the then condition of artillery and naval armaments. The Emperor did not live to see the completion of this Cyclopean work; but his famous phrase, " I had resolved to repeat at Cherbourg the marvels of Egypt ", has justly been carved on the pedestal of his equestrian statue, pointing towards England with upraised arm.

The plan conceived in the xviiith century could not be fully carried into effect till the Second Empire; but it was inspired by the genius of Napoleon. Long-range artillery and dreadnoughts have since upset all calculations, but Cherbourg, where, as elsewhere, this has been taken into account, is still formidable. It is a very great arsenal and dockyard, a safe roadstead, and one of the most important home ports for Trans-atlantic liners. From the top of the precipitous slopes of Mont Le Roule, crowned by a fort, there is a splendid view over the country, the neigh-bouring watering-places, the open sea and the town. The latter is dull and formal, and its chief attraction is a visit to the military port. It has, however, a museum of paintings, presented and organised by Thomas

Henry, in which are to be found some excellent works, chief among which is an exquisite series of bas-reliefs by the great Clodion, the French della Robbia, and some pictures by Roger van der Weyden, Ghirlandajo, Poussin, Chardin, Ribera, Boilly, Panini, Pourbus, Greuze... A pleasant surprise awaits the visitor in this gallery, which is far superior to many a better-known provincial museum.

Cherbourg is a bathing-place only for its own inhabitants, but its immediate surroundings are very picturesque, and often of striking beauty. At the very extremity of this point of the Cotentin one can still find one's ideal, which is growing more and more rare; namely, a really simple seaside place, where one can lead a life free from all snobbish conventions, in the heart of nature, and accomplish the miracle of eating, in full view of the waves, as much fish as one likes, — a thing hardly to be found along the whole coast of the Channel, to the exasperation of visitors. The peninsula of La Hague is wonderful. Its great silent heaths, purple with their thick carpet of heather, and blazing with golden broom, give it even here the character of Brittany. Here we already find those tawny rocks, with their distorted outlines, which give austere Armorica its beauty, and which one seeks in vain on the Norman coast between

Between Omonville-la-Rogue and Auderville.

here and Etretat. It is a sombre region, as yet unprofaned by tourists and a public greedy for vulgar amusements. Here there are no odious casinos or regiments of bathing-huts; but its attraction for painters is strong. May such corners as lovely Landemer, hidden in its hollow valley, remain for a long time comparatively deserted ! And near at hand, in the country, is Gréville, with its old church, half-Romanesque, half-Gothic, whose image has been piously reproduced in a little masterpiece, preserved in the Louvre, by the genius of François Millet, who was born in a cottage in the hamlet of Gruchy. When one succeeds in finding a conveyance, or bravely sets out on foot, by a road whose beauty would be a recompense for many fatigues, past the old cabaret called " The Bacchus "; or when, by way of Beaumont, one reaches the grottoes and the strange cliff known as the Nez de Jobourg, rising 420 feet above a stormy sea bristling with reefs; when at last one walks out on to the point of

Gréville. The Church.

La Hague, from which one can see Aurigny floating on the vast sea, one is held fast by the majestic melancholy of the place, and realises how far one is from what the fashionable world of Deauville, or the good people at middle-class seaside resorts, understand by " going to the seaside ". And one also realises why the Normans of the districts of Auge and the Virois are of opinion that the Cotentin is and yet is not Normandy.

The Co-
tentin is, in
fact, a land
apart, of an
exceptional
character.
Though the
magnificent
cliffs of Dié-
lette and Fla-
manville have
been disembo
welled by the
workings of the

A House at Landemer.

quarries and iron mines which are gradually spoiling these places, the
seaside resorts which one passes as one goes southwards along the coast
have all remained faithful to a healthily natural, simple and elemental life
which the fashionable bathing places have obliterated almost everywhere
else, by transforming the seaside resorts into offshoots of the boulevard.
How graceful are the little old ports of Carteret and Portbail, where
one can really watch the life of the fishermen! And here, beside the
restless, tragic sea, the climate of the country is already curiously
mild, as in Brittany, and one is astonished to find flowers and fig-trees
which can stand the winter. Coutances has its neighbouring watering
places; Coutainville, Agon, Régnéville, and Montmartin. Granville raises
proudly on its rock the martial old city which the English bombarded
many a time, and
to which the army
of the Vendée
under La Rochejac-
quelein laid siege
in vain. From the
port of Granville
went forth many of
those rude corsairs
who, like the men
of Dieppe and St.
Malo, gave chase to
the ships of Great
Britain during

Gréville. Statue of Millet.

Sunset at Granville.

many centuries. And finally, Avranches too has its seaside places, calm and exquisitely pretty, which one reaches by traversing a fruitful country-side Jullonville, Saint-Pair, Genêts, from whence one begins to see Mont St. Michel.

But if we wish to understand the grave and poetic, if wild character of the Cotentin, it must be looked for inland, between Coutances and Valognes. M. René Bazin has recently employed his emotional mastery and reverent understanding of peasant customs and character in describing these places. But we should turn to Barbey d'Aurevilly

Granville.

even more than to him. This great and profoundly Norman writer has
sought in this region the background for more than one of his novels. He has
in particular given powerful expression to the fantastic character of the
vast heath of Lessay, extending from La Haye du Puits to the outskirts
of Coutances, near the two old villages of Lessay and Périers, whose two
Gothic churches, and especially the latter, with its imposing beauty,

Pointe de la Hague.

evoke the memory of the Benedictines. A once famous fair, which is still
largely frequented, takes place on the edge of this heath, whose silence
it breaks once a year. It is a sort of desert space in the midst of this
fruitful countryside of the Cotentin, a kind of Norman Crau, in which
the mirage and the extreme solitude have given rise to many legends of
ghosts, as in the wilder parts of Brittany. The most cheerful traveller
dreads crossing the heath of Lessay; though at the same time it is loved
for its mysterious poetry, which has inspired the heart-stirring *complaintes,*
of many local bards.

Valognes, in the very heart of the Cotentin, is a little viscounty,
deserted and fallen from its former state. It is also an ancient fortress,
the former Alaunia of the Gallo-Romans, which long boasted a ceremo
nious and pretentious nobility, a laughing-stock of the xviiith century.
These ruined nobles have gradually died out, and no trace of them remains

save their mansions, which are crumbling away in their deserted state.
Valognes is sad and mute, but an artist could go there to find health by
steeping himself in silence. Men of worth have been born there. Letourneur,
who made a conscientious translation of Shakespeare, Vicq d'Azyr,
Dacier, Burnouf, Léopold Delisle, and near by, at St. Sauveur-le-Vicomte,
Barbey d'Aurevilly, that great and faithful poet of the Norman land,
who has given in many of his novels descriptions of
Valognes which possess the rare and magic power of calling

up, over and above its external features, the soul of the
place described. Saint-Lô,
quite near Coutances on the
east, is likewise built on a
rock, which enabled the
sans-culottes to christen it
"Rocher de la Liberté"; but
it soon resumed its ancient
name, which was that of one
of its children in the vith century, Laudus, Laud or Lô,
who became Bishop of Cou-
tances, and whose relics
returned to his native place.
Saint-Lô, which was a fortified town, saw some bloody
days during the struggles
of the Reformation, and in
particular the terrible massacre of 1574, in which the
Catholics avenged themselves on the Calvinists. Saint-

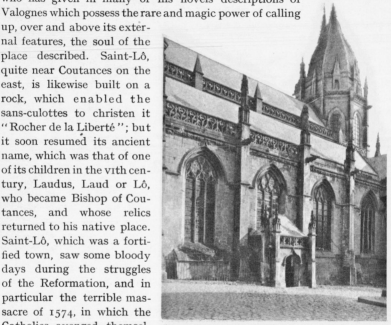

Valognes. The Dome of the Church.

Lô is dominated by a very imposing cathedral, half flamboyant, half
Gothic, full of delightful detail. In this town, the birthplace of the
astronomer Le Verrier and of the novelist Octave Feuillet, there is a
museum which, among a few tolerable pictures, has the honour to hold
Corot's *Homer and the Shepherds*, a work in which the calm majesty of
Poussin is already allied with the divinely tender naturalism of the
most touching of our poet-painters. This perfect masterpiece would in
itself make a visit to Saint-Lô worth while, quite as much as the celebrated breeding-stables, or the famous Gallo-Roman inscription on red

marble, found at Torigny-sur-Vire by the Matignon family, and given to the Town Hall of Saint-Lô by the ancestors of the present princes of Mondeo. But in order to love Saint-Lô, all that is necessary is to seek and find in it the charm of those little cities in which one wanders at large and lives at ease in calm and healthy spots.

Travelling through rich lands, dotted with attractive country towns and estates, where one would be glad to live, we reach Coutances, the gentle rival of Avranches, for which it seems to furnish the model. Like Avranches and Saint-Lô, it is built on a granite pro-montory, lower and less precipi-tous than theirs.

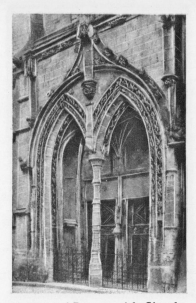

Valognes. A Doorway of the Church.

It was the Cosedia of the Gauls. Fortified by Constantius Chlorus, it took its name from him. Cosedia became Constantia, then Coutances. It suggested the name of the whole region, for the Cotentin, formerly called Costentin, is the " Constantine " province. Less fortunate than Avranches, Coutances had to suffer many assaults. It was taken and re-taken in those far distant days when the sons of William the Conqueror, Rufus and Curthose, began their clumsy struggle against the covetousness of those beyond the Channel for the heritage of their father. The same happened at the time of the Hundred Years' War and the Wars of Religion, though Matignon, the clever governor, managed to spare it a share in the effects of the horrible massacre of St. Bartholomew. The disorders of the Barefoot insurrection extended as far as Coutances. Like Avranches, it numbered a saint among its bishops. With Saint-Lô it can proudly compare Saint Aubert, who gave his name to a neighbouring town. It has even a local

Saint-Lô. Détail of the Cathedral.

Château de Vauville.

heroine, Jeanne Paynel, who joined the knights of the Sire d'Estouteville when they went to defend Mont St-Michel against the attacks of the English. Nowadays Coutances, with a population of less than seven thousand, is placidity itself. It would be hard to find a more softly pleasing little town. A hill covered with houses standing in gardens, arranged along the fine, sloping, silent boulevards, rises out of the foliage, and presents, as if in a basket of flowers, its cathedral of Notre-Dame, one of the finest on French soil. Archaeologists have disputed a great deal over its date. It was probably built in the xith century and remodelled and enlarged in the xiiith, without its being thought necessary to ruin its first style by its second, which has been fused with the earlier one without supplanting it. In it

Bay of Vauville.

Gothic and Romanesque are mingled with harmonious elegance in every part of the building, of which the two towers over the doorway and the central tower with its lantern, are masterpieces of religious architecture. This richly carved mass regally dominates Coutances. Notre-Dame would make one forget the Church of St. Pierre, near at hand, which can show a very fine flamboyant Gothic tower and central tower of the Renaissance period Lastly, Coutances has a charming public garden, as shady and ornate as could be desired, where a monument to the great aesthetician Remy de Gourmont has recently been raised by the pious care of men of letters. But this garden does not look out on an enchanting view like its rival at Avranches.

Coutances. Wells of Our Lady in the Cathedral.

Avranches is on the boundary between the Norman and Breton territories. A few kilometres to the west, and we come to Pontorson and Dol, the cradle of Duguesclin and the fringe of Armorica. From Avranches one can almost descry St. Malo and Cancale. But Avranches is also the foundation of the Cotentin, shaped like the tower of a fortress outlined against the sea. Avranches is a restful and charming town. It rises on a steep hill in the midst of the most smiling of landscapes. At the foot of the hill winds the silvery Sée, through meadows

Avranches. The Cathedral.

fringed with grey willows, or salt-marshes of sandy mud *(tangue)* on which are grazed the sheep whose mutton is known as *pré-salé*, and where wild geese disport themselves, which are poor eating but are bred for the sake of their down, from which are made those luxurious feather beds which are the pride of provincial bedchambers. Avranches is the old city of the Gaulish tribe of the Abrincates, but has only played a very modest part in history. The most salient fact in its history was a sort of Jacquerie which took place in 1639 and was known as the Bare-foot insurrection *(Révolte des Nu-Pieds)*, a revolt of the peasants against the salt-tax. It was a terrible revolt, commanded by Jean Nu-Pieds, the leader, and the priest Morel, and it took a military expedition under Marshal Gassion to put an end to it by a process of extermination, after terrible scenes. It was at Avranches that Saint-Aubert, one of its bishops, gave the order to found on the slopes of Mont St-Michel the humble oratory which was to grow into such a strong and

In the Gardens of Avranches.

Coutances. The Cathedral.

famous edifice. Since the Revolution Avranches has had no bishop, and its fine episcopal palace, with its noble garden, is occupied by the law-courts. The churches of Saint-Gervais and Notre-Dame-des-Champs are modern copies of the Gothic or early Renaissance style, and the *sous-préfecture* and Town Hall are quiet and ordinary. The streets are fringed by grey stone houses, respectable and solid; the museum is of small account. But there are the Botanical Gardens with their soft charm, an oasis of tranquil grace, with their magnificent trees, their flower-beds and ornamental vases arranged with perfect taste. It is the only smiling corner in a city as melancholy as all Norman provincial towns, and like the silent *place* before the *sous-préfecture*, only with a wider expanse, it overlooks a splendid landscape of trees, shore and sea; while on the horizon rises the distant outline of Mont St-Michel, looking quite unreal, as if hanging between sky and sea. And so sleepy Avranches, like a nest of secluded lives, hangs on the edge of an empty immensity. And I recommend it as a dreaming-place for the remaining few who understand the ecstasy of musing on this terrace in the morning or at twilight.

Bay of Mont Saint-Michel. A washing Place.

Bay of Mont Saint-Michel from the Gardens of Avranches.

CHAPTER VIII

—

Mont Saint-Michel

Before we approach Mont St-Michel, it is doubtless preferable to have our first vision of it from afar. Of all points of view the best is that from the terrace of the Botanical Gardens overlooking Avranches.

A vast expanse lies spread out before us. On the right is Normandy, verdant and fruitful, with its rich meadows and bluish forests, all the planes of the landscape harmonising in a perfect rhythmical balance. On the left, the estuary of the Sée stretches out its grey mud flats between wooded tongues of land and little fantastically shaped capes, with the river winding through it all like

Mont Saint-Michel. (Detail).

gleaming silver. Thanks to the refraction of light and the increasing distance, all this silver and grey merges into a vast area of diffused lights, in which the dazzled eye can no longer distinguish the water from the land and sky. It is all made up of tremulous lights, vague forms, mirage and reflected gleams. But in the centre of this vaporous illusion there rises up a strange pyramid. Alone in the immensity, rising out of the waves, solid, real, and yet inexplicable,

Saint-Léonard. Maison de Chaume.

it lifts up its pointed mass, and the eye distinguishes by degrees a pile of enormous blocks, a leafy wood, fortifications, the nave of a church, a devotional building perched upon a military one, a spire on whose point there trembles a little ray of gold. According to the play of sun and cloud, this pyramid is sometimes tawny, sometimes pink, sometimes black like a mass of basalt. It lies there like a fantastic ship at anchor. Behind it on the horizon, as far as the eye can reach, lies a curving shore, flat or broken by the crests of forests, melting into the sky, fading away in tones of slaty grey, in a subtle mingling of greenish or mauve-

Saint-Léonard. The Church.

tinted blues. Some way towards the north-east is a rock like a crouching
beast, or stranded monster, which seems to keep watch over this mo-
tionless ship Such is the aspect of Mont St-Michel and Tombelaine, as
they lie off the Breton shore, in the midst of a bay whose mouth, from
Cancale to Granville, measures eight leagues, while it is hollowed out
to an equal depth up to the threshold of Avranches. But even when

Mont Saint-Michel.

one knows it is all there, one thinks that it is all a dream, and that the
impression will vanish with the ray of light which evoked it.

Round the coasts of the bay, on the Breton, as on the Norman side,
certain points give one a nearer view of this pyramid, which seems almost
to have fallen from high heaven upon this tideless sea The best of these
are undoubtedly the old village of Saint-Léonard, with its exquisite
crumbling priory and its little cottages, a peaceful refuge for the artist or
the poet; and that charming seaside place Genêts, with its weatherbeaten
church in a pure Gothic style, from whence a regular service of covered
wagons runs to and from the Mount, across the sands, at low tide. Before
the embankment was constructed, along which a steam tramway runs
from Pontorson and communicates with the Mount, the carts from Genêts
were the only means of access to the colossal fortress-church. They are

Mont Saint-Michel. The East Part.

still much used, and their course is carefully marked out. Improvident travellers have often perished by venturing on to the quicksands which shift with the tides — those beds of *tangue*, a grey mud which dries quickly in the free air which blows into the bay, and fertilizes the whole region, where flocks of wild geese fly high above innumerable grazing sheep.

This *tangue*, streaked by the freshwater rills of the Sée, the Sélune and the Couesnon, and by the pools left by the retreating sea, creates a landscape recalling the Dutch polders, with their splendid moisture-laden skies and palaces of cloud poetically rendered by Van Goyen and Ruysdael. When the sea comes rushing into the Bay at an incredible speed, covering the ground with silver and pearl, the sheep are hastily shut up in the farms; and at the spring tides a violent tidal wave rushes far inland up the sluggish Couesnon, and the waves foam at the foot of the hill of Avranches.

From Genêts it is less than 4 miles to the Mount, which no longer looks like a phantom vision. One can appreciate the architectural detail of the buildings upon it, its vast size, its powerful solidity, the heroic proportions of this mass, like a wild beast at rest, relaxing a moment only to soar suddenly skywards. And one is struck by a double sensation;

that of the force of nature and of human audacity seen side by side, the one, by an act of will, at once obeying and dominating the other. The dour Gothic genius, tameless, yet illuminated by faith, recalls to our minds the centuries of mighty effort of the Assyrians and Egyptians. Here is the same mystery as to the means employed — means which were wretched compared with ours, yet managed to effect what our " progress " falls so short even of attempting; the same mystery as to the anonymous artists who conceived and carried out this work, unique in the world. The history of the Mount is the history of an idea, pursued throughout the needs and transformations of the centuries. Nature, by some strange whim, has cast this mass of stone down in the midst of the estuary, this granite block, on the north side of which thick vegetation has sprung up; a block as abnormal in this place as its neighbour Tombelaine. The earliest

men rightly compared them both to sepulchres in the midst of the waves, and the Celts imagined that it was to islands such as those off the Channel coasts and the Channel Islands that the souls of the dead, gathered together in the boat of a supernatural ferryman, like the Charon of the Greeks, came to seek their last rest far from the living. Such was the destiny which the Breton Chateaubriand desired for his soul, when he wished to be buried near St-Malo, on the Grand Bé. The larger of these two blocks was first called the Mont Tombe, and the other Tombelaine — the little tomb. But soon came Christianity, and with it

A Street in Mont Saint-Michel.

a miracle. In the viiith century Saint Aubert, Bishop of Avranches, saw St. Michael appear to him and order him to found an oratory at the foot of the pyramid of the Mont Tombe. Aubert obeyed, copying the oratory which the Italian monks had hollowed out in honour of the Archangel in the side of Mount Gargano, as a result of a similar apparition. From this time onwards the name of St. Michael was attached to this wild spot.

Two hundred years later, a Carlovingian church took the place of the humble oratory hollowed out in the rock. When the Northmen came, it was necessary to fortify the base of the Mount, in order to protect it from pillage; and a certain number of the shore population took refuge with the monks in order to escape from the pirates who were ravaging the coast. There they built themselves houses haphazard, and a village sprang up. Later on Richard I, the descendant of the Vikings, became Duke of Normandy, and sent the Benedictines to the Mount to found an Abbey, when a Romanesque basilica was substituted for the Carlovingian church. When Philip Augustus took possession of the Duchy, he sent troops who failed to oust the Normans, but set fire to the place. Once master of the land, the King of France at once gave the monks the means to rebuild, in even finer style, the buildings which had been destroyed·

Salle des Chevaliers.

Mont Saint-Michel. The Cloisters.

The Chapter House.

This was the origin of the monastery, built in twenty-five years, between 1203 and 1228, which bears and merits in the eyes of all the name of La Merveille — the Marvel. At his accession St. Louis made a still greater offering to it, and gave orders that the Mount should be transformed into a monastery and fortress combined. Round it was built that mighty array of towers and ramparts which time has left untouched. The garrison was supported by the king and the monastery, under the command of the abbot, who was also the royal governor; while the work of constructing and adorning the buildings went on continually. The ancient Tomb had become the centre of the famous pilgrimage of Saint-Michel-au-péril-de-la-Mer. Later on, during the Hundred Years' War, the military art of the xivth century remodelled the defences, which were considered inadequate, completing and strengthening the formidable crenellated outer wall. Twice did the English attempt to storm this fortified sanctuary. They had taken up their position on Tombelaine, but were ousted from it by a squadron sent from Saint-Malo in 1423. They returned eleven years later, and got as far as the enceinte; but the garrison hurled them back towards the sea, and they fled, leaving behind them two massive bombards, the " Michelettes ", which are still to be seen at the entrance to the citadel, with their great stone cannon-balls beside them.

The reign of Louis XI marks the height of the wealth and prestige of the Mount, to which resorted innumerable pilgrims. In 1469 the King created the knightly Order of St. Michael, and the new dignitaries held their first session in the great hall of the monastery, which became the hall of honour of the knights. The age of the Wars of Religion revived the same perils as had threatened the Mount in the Hundred Years' War. It withstood several attacks, notably that of Montgomery in 1591, but its walls remained inviolate. But decadence overtook the place. The abbots overstepped their rights, the monks, isolated in this half-military life, lost the fervour of their predecessors. They were replaced in the xviith century by the monks of Saint-Maur; and later the Kings sent political prisoners to the Mount, which from the Revolution till the last few years of the Second Empire, was transformed into a house of detention for agitators like Barbès and Blanqui. It was the Third Republic which abolished this dismal and unworthy way of using the old sanctuary, declared the Mount to be a historical monument, effaced the traces of the vandalism of its gaolers and garrison, and called upon the sculptor Fremiet to model a St. Michael with the dragon to adorn its dizzy spire. This fine, noble statue of ruddy bronze gleams at a height of 500 feet above the expanse of the sea; and it was the glitter of the golden rays reflected from it which we saw from the terrace at Avranches. The archangel dominates, protects and gives his benediction to the vast sweep of the bay like a symbol of the triumph of spirit over matter, and of faith over the blind forces

The Crypt.

of the sea. But indeed the whole Mount is a symbol of this spiritual triumph.

There is one hard fact to which all travellers who are lovers of art and dreams are bound to resign themselves. There is no famous place in the world, be it cathedral, museum or palace, which does not attract the ordinary tourist, and one has to listen to the comments of a noisy curiosity, often stupid and sometimes irreverent. This suffering imposed upon those enthusiastic souls who can grasp the majesty of the place, and would wish to save it from insult and venerate it in isolation, is the price they have to pay for their pure emotions. Mont Saint-Michel is no exception to this general law. It is invaded by careless and idle sight-seers, like Venice, like Florence, like all great and beautiful places born of nature and of human genius. We must of course resign ourselves; but we need not draw too melancholy a con-

The lace-work Stairway.

clusion as to the profanation of the Merveille. Enclosed within its Cyclopean walls it soars too high to be spoilt. The crowds of motors which stand along the shores, overshadowed by its great mass and lost in this vast landscape, produce no more effect than so many tiny crabs at the foot of a cliff; and if one is wise, one cheerfully makes the best of the crowd which jostles along the one street of the village. This street, which

The Cloisters.

rises steeply up, with its tiring cobblestones, narrow and bordered by houses of the xvth century, looks like the scenery of an opera full of a crowd of supers without stage costumes. It also reminds one of an Oriental street in an Exhibition, with its innumerable awnings, so nearly meeting that they hide the sky, beneath which are crowded booths full of postcards, pottery and trifles. After all, it is an amusing sight, with its open air clatter and its frank commercialism. But if the visitor is offended by it, he has only to take a few steps to find himself behind the houses, on the mighty ramparts deserted by the customers of the booths, before the incomparable view of the incoming tide, or of the shores with their strange silvery pallor. Besides, there is the promise of the evening, when the art-loving traveller is sure to enjoy almost alone the emotions which come with nightfall, when the moon shines over the waves, in this lovely setting where the soul of the Mystic Past is revived, amid the fairy-like beauty of the sea.

The great cities of modern times extend horizontally. Mediaeval cities extended vertically, for reasons of military protection. On the summit of the elevated sites, chosen because of the difficulty of scaling them, and the facilities which they gave for scanning the horizon — crowded within a strong system of ramparts which its limited area enabled to be held by a small body of men, they piled up their houses on successive levels round the central stronghold and the church, whose spire, planted like a mast in the structure of a ship, scattered its prayers and its knell through the wide heavens. And so the Mount brings together all the elements of a town upon its rock about half a mile round, a stone vessel anchored in a desert of water; and, as on board a ship, the smallest space is cleverly utilised, and no additions could be made to it except by extending it upwards. Hence the necessity of the miracle of the Merveille, by which the Abbey is built with gigantic foundations upon which are superimposed the guard-room, the hall of the knights, the monastery, and the church, in three stone stories, sometimes of weathered stone, sometimes carved with all the delicacy of a light wisp of lace. It is this accumulation, disciplined by this order, which remains the secret of the genius of Gothic builders.

In this material Marvel is contained the further marvel of the cohesion of idea and form; and it stands indestructible. Neither the religious disaffection of the present day nor the idle curiosity of visitors can impair the solemnity and grandeur of such a masterpiece. Mont St-Michel marks the boundary between Normandy and Brittany, outlined by the course of the Couesnon, which dies away in the sand at its feet. It looks out over them both, but it stands firm on Norman soil. Its history is bound up with that of Normandy, and it is, with the cathedral of Rouen, the peerless jewel of the Norman treasury.

Chapel of Mont Saint-Michel. The Four Evangelists.

A Normandy Landscape.

—

CHAPTER IX

Central Normandy and the Norman Switzerland

When we leave the neighbourhood of Avranches and Mont St-Michel, and turn eastwards, the southern zone of Normandy presents quite a different appearance from that of the plateau of Caux, the plains of Caen and the Bessin, the heaths of the Cotentin, or the rich meadows, pastures and fields of the districts of Auge or the Bocage. We find ourselves in a picturesque and irregular country, with rocky hills, from which we can look out on a series of wide views, with deep, dark forests and a hilly character, whose irregularities and woodland appearance have won for certain parts of it the name of the Norman Switzerland. This is the region whose appearance undergoes a series of changes from Avranches to Mortain and Vire, to Domfront and Falaise, to

Mortain. Waterfalls of the Cance.

the Forest of Andaine and Bagnoles, the Argentan and Alençon, and the imaginary frontier of the province slants north-eastwards through Mortagne to Laigle, Verneuil, Conches and Evreux, thus completing the circuit of our imaginary journey. The name of Norman Switzerland is actually more suited to the region of Mortain, Domfront and Bagnoles; but it is also claimed by that central section, in the upper valley of the Orne to the south of Caen, which stretche from Clécy to Flers by way of Thury-Harcourt and Condé-sur-Noireau, and of which Falaise on its rock is the eastern outpost. Seaside visitors who think they know Normandy because they have seen Dieppe, Fécamp, Honfleur, Cherbourg or Granville — even those who have visited Rouen, Lisieux or Caen — have no idea of the configu-

Mortain. Houses.

The Cance at Mortain.

ration and atmosphere of southern Normandy, bordering on the Perche, Sarthe, Eure and Loir. It is a country apart, with a soul apart.

Mortain is the first town which one comes to as one travels eastwards

Vire.

from Avranches. It is quite a little town without a history, though the countship of Mortain was an appanage of the Anglo-Norman dynasty from the days of the Conqueror till the second half of the xvth century, and gave rise to many an armed struggle. It consists of hardly more than one long street, in which the sole building of interest is the old Gothic church of Saint-Evroult. One has to climb up to the Chapel of St-Michel and the Rocks of Montjoie in order to grasp the full beauty of the setting which nature has been pleased to give to Mortain, with its houses ranged in a long line above the deep rocky bed of the Cance, which, like all the neighbouring rivers, carves out a southward course through the granite on its way to the Mayenne, outside the borders of Normandy. This outlying region of Mortain is the paradise of artists who paint forest landscapes. The forest-clad hills rise one beyond the other to the extreme limits of the horizon, and one can still distinguish the vaporous outline of Mont Saint-Michel, ten leagues away. From the door of the old " Abbaye

Blanche " the view is just as fine, and on the side of the valley opposite Mortain is the Neufbourg, overlooking those wonders of nature, the Little Cascade and the Great Cascade, formed by the waters of the Cance as they rush headlong downwards, breaking in rainbow spray. M. René Bazin has described these waterfalls with that great and sincere love of nature which glows in the fine talent with which he describes landscapes in prose. And he justly remarks that besides these cascades, which are comparable with those of Switzerland and the Pyrenees, though less famous, the whole valley of the Cance, with Mortain itself and its gorge, is a pure delight for poets and painters. Why has the Mortainais not had its Lamartine and its Corot? But it is enough to have

Vire. The Belfry.

a sensitive nature, capable of experiencing emotion in the presence of the grace and majesty of this spot, in order to love this corner of France, which is among its most beautiful, if least renowned.

If we return northwards, and pass from Manche into Orne, in the direction of Vire, we reach this town by travelling, as it were, through one vast, continuous orchard of apple-trees. On leaving the irregular landscape of Mortain, we find ourselves in the heart of the Bocage. But Vire, like Mortain, Coutances and Avranches, is also perched on top of a steep hill, surrounded by the river of the same name. And here we again come

Vire. The Cathedral and the Rue de la Boucherie.

upon memories of feudal days. It was near Vire, at Tinchebray, that Robert Curthose, the incompetent younger son of the Conqueror, was beaten and deprived of his duchy by Henry I of England, at the beginning of the xIIth century. William's work was not long in falling to pieces; and Henry was careful to found on this spot a fortress which passed later into the hands of the Kings of France. At Vire are to be found many traces of the ramparts built by the English. There is nothing remarkable about the church; but one can still see there some amusing old houses and a fifteenth century bell tower. One has the pleasure of finding in the little museum a Poussin, a Chardin, some pictures by Theodore Rousseau and Paul Huet, Corot, Troyon and Daubigny. But the charm of Vire lies in its delightful surroundings, its gardens, and its points of view, from which one can see, in particular, the famous Valleys of Vire

(Vaux de Vire). They are nothing but one pretty winding valley; but they have given their name, as everyone knows, to those " vaudevilles ", or songs making fun of the powers that be, which express the ironical humour of the men of Vire, and were collected and enriched with his own mocking genius by the local poet Olivier Basselin.

Domfront also forms part of a series of towns perched on top of that long sandstone ridge, which is, as it were, a continuation of the geological character of Brittany into this southwestern region of Normandy. Domfront was an ancient group of primitive dwellings which

Domfront.

gathered in the vith century round a hut built in this wild spot by the hermit known later as Saint Front — *dominus Frons.* Situated as it was on a rocky crest which is hard to climb, cut by a deep gorge, 230 feet deep, at the bottom of which babbles the river Varenne, it could hardly fail to be chosen for the erection of a fortress. William of Alençon built one there at the beginning of the xiith century and the group of huts became a little citadel. It was often besieged. The Wars of Religion raged around it. It was here that the career of the adventurous Montgomery, a Calvinist captain whose exploits and

Domfront. The Château.

cruelties have left many traces in Normandy, came to an end. Forced to surrender to Marshal Matignon, he gave himself up; but he was too inconvenient to Queen Catherine de' Medici for her to deprive herself of the pleasure of having him beheaded, in spite of the terms of the capitulation. This siege was the last page in the history of picturesque Domfront. The castle is the only point of notable interest, but, ruined as it is, it is still formidable, lying outside the town, which was itself enclosed within rough walls with twenty-four towers, which are still visible.

The weathering of centuries and the rampant vegetation have transformed these venerable and heroic ramparts into a poem of picturesque decay to which no description can do justice. But one forgets them when one looks out over the amazing landscape round, extending from the forests of the Mortainais to the Forest of Andaine, whose mysterious

Bagnoles-de-l'Orne.

blues were so dear to Remy de Gourmont. It is indeed rare in France to
meet with visions of more majestic harmony than those which stretch
before the art-lover who looks down, as from a balcony, from these little
silent towns, Avranches, Mortain or Domfront. The rugged nobility of
Brittany is here united with the soft fruitfulness of Normandy, and out
of these hills of moderate height, never exceeding 1150 feet, and
these modest streams such as the Sélune, the Sée, the Cance or the
Varenne, nature achieves the miracle of composing landscapes which
are impressive, and sometimes even savage. The series of them con-
tinues, ever offering fresh beauties, as far as Bagnoles, beyond the
9 miles of the Forest of Andaine. Through a cleft in the granite
ridge which is continued here from Mortain, the little river Vée
winds along, flowing round Bagnoles and forming a lake. The charming
situation of Bagnoles has justly been compared to that of Spa or the
watering-places of the Vosges, but it has an attraction all its own and
thoroughly Norman, in the rich softness of its foliage, the amenity of its
climate, and that tranquillity which lays its stamp upon the elegance
of its luxurious villas, lying among the rocks, the fir-trees, and the parks
full of flowers. Nowhere are there more interesting, pretty and healthy

walks to be found than those in the immediate neighbourhood of Bagnoles and its suburb Tessé-la-Madeleine.

From this point we can once more interrupt our eastward course round the outer circuit of Normandy and make a rapid detour towards the centre, descending the course of the Orne in order to reach an equally pretty region. The district lying between Vire and Falaise also aspires to the name of the Norman Switzerland, claimed by the Mortainais, and is indeed not unworthy of it. History, it is true, has no rights here; and though the Norman warriors in chain mail, and the wandering bands of the League, certainly marched along its roads, ill-treating the villagers here as everywhere, no traces of them have remained. There is nothing to be said about Condé-sur-Noireau, except that the famous Dumont d'Urville was born there. Nor have Clécy and Thury-Harcourt — with its fine XVIIth century château — a long list of warlike feats to show, of sieges ending, in correct fashion, in stormings, sackings and burnings — in fact in all the prestige of a historic triumph. But what delightful little spots they are ! How pleasant life is here, on the banks of the silvery Orne, among the rocky hills with their green summits. Here the lover of nature, the dreamer, the jaded worker longing for grateful silence, can be certain of finding the most delicious of French oases. Here that expression of

The Orne at Condé.

Falaise.

" Old France ", dear to us above all others, with its promise of tranquil

Falaise. The Arlette Fountain.

harmony, takes on its full meaning. It is true that this little annexe of the Norman Switzerland, next door to the Bocage, with its sombre beech woods, its apple orchards and granite rocks, is less grand and irregular than the region between Mortain and Domfront. But its modest proportions lend it, perhaps, a more intimate charm. Clécy is fairly well frequented by painters. Nowadays it has become the fashion to compose landscapes which have only a very indirect relation with the observation of nature. " Synthesis " is the catch-word, and the task of expressing natural beauty as it is is left contemptuously to photography. But it may be regretted that at the period when artists like Theodore Rousseau, Daubigny and Corot were content to be

Falaise. Statue of William the Conqueror.

" photographers ", by virtue of the pious care with which they painted rocks and trees, such spots as these did not create a Norman school as rich as that of Fontainebleau. It is true that there have been many painters of the Norman countryside, who have loved their little fatherland and devoted themselves to the task of expressing it; and in all the local museums one often finds canvasses of considerable merit, signed by painters like Motelay, Tesnières and R. Morel-Fatio, who have not greatly cared to seek fame in Paris, and whose names the art-loving traveller learns with surprise and pleasure. None of them, however, was great, and when one thinks of the famous group who produced so many masterpieces in the region of Barbizon, one laments the absence of those which might have been inspired by landscapes as fine as those of the Mortainais, of Domfront, the Bocage, and the upper valley of the Orne.

Séez.

A short détour to the east from the neighbourhood of Clécy will bring us to Falaise. This is one the most important towns in the national history, for it was here that William the Conqueror was born. His ducal ancestors had already fortified it and chosen it for their favourite residence. Perhaps its castle was completed and embellished by Duke Robert the Magnificent. This duke was none other than the famous Robert the Devil. Legend has endowed him with a thousand misdeeds which cannot be proved, but have brought him notoriety, and also the privilege of being the hero of Meyerbeer's most ill-natured opera. This terrible duke, looking out of his castle windows, saw a pretty girl washing clothes, on the banks of the Ante. She was the daughter of a tanner of Falaise. He took a fancy to her, and before long she bore a son. No doubt such events were not rare between him and his young subjects; but this time the idyll was of some importance, for the child who was born was William the Bastard. He was recognised by his father and was destined to become first heir to the duchy, which he was able to defend against rival barons,

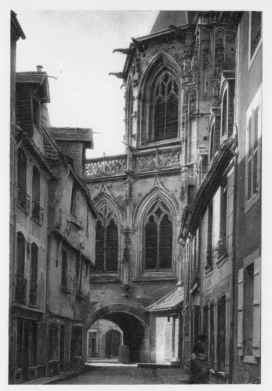

Falaise. Church of the Trinity.

and then the conqueror of Harold the Saxon and the founder of modern England. This affair, which brought Robert the Devil's misdeeds to such a glorious end, and turned him respectable through the agency of the beautiful Arlette, is related with the addition of many details at the castle of Falaise; and it is pleasant to accept it in the form in which it is told, as one visits the " Fountain of Arlette ", and even the little room in which she visited her ducal lover, a room hollowed out in the walls, which are some twelve feet thick. This castle, like all those of the period, was not very pleasant-looking, but they did not spare the stone in building it. It raises its formidable bulk and its sixteen towers, adorned with splendid lime-trees, with as much majesty as the Keep of Gisors. The interior is ruined and roofless, but the general shape of the outside is almost intact, and produces a heroic impression when it is seen from the town which it commands. It goes without saying that this castle, like the Bayeux Tapestry and the memorial column at Dives, is naturally an object of curiosity to innumerable English visitors. Falaise is a regular Mecca to them. It is a pretty little city, with its fine Gothic church of La Trinité and from almost all its streets one catches a glimpse of attrac-

A Normandy Landscape.

tive views and characteristic aspects of the country, towards the Brèche au Diable, the banks of the Laize or the Vale of Ussy.

And so we return towards Argentan and Alençon. Argentan, the birthplace of the historian Mézeray, a charming city without a history, is mirrored in the Orne, with its silvery gleams like those beloved of Corot. Here we find the remains of a castle and fortifications, and two churches which would have every claim to be considered remarkable if

Fresnay-sur-Sarthe.

one did not become more and more exacting in the course of such a

Saint-Céneri.

journey : Saint Germain and Saint Martin, both in the flamboyant style and well-preserved. Charming churches like these cannot stand beside the great masterpieces of Rouen, Caen, Bayeux and Coutances. But we must be ready with a just tribute of affection for the exquisite little town of Séez. It is of venerable antiquity, and has been the seat of a bishopric since the ivth century. In later days the Northmen destroyed its abbey of Saint-Martin, which was piously restored in the xiith century by a Montgomery. And five hundred years later, another Montgomery attacked it — that fierce and famous Protestant leader who laid waste so many Norman towns before he was captured by Matignon at the siege of Domfront. He sacked Séez, but spared the abbey, though consecrated to the Popery which he hated, because his ancestor had rebuilt it. Séez is a silent city in a soft and smiling countryside, near the great Forest of Ecouves, abounding in lovely prospects. It nestles in the shadow of a cathedral of St. Gervais and St. Protais, which is one of the mightiest achievements of Norman religious architecture, a masterpiece of the great builder, John of Bernières. The friable character of the soil has unfortunately rendered necessary an incessant task of consolidating and repairing this majestic church, the interior of which is perfectly beautiful, though out of all proportion to the size of Séez, now so quiet and almost deserted.

Alençon is the chief town of the department of Orne, one of the five departments known as Norman. But here we are at the extreme southern limit of Normandy, on the outskirts of Sarthe, a region of quite a different character. A few steps further, and we should step quite outside the plan of this book. And yet the Conqueror has left his mark here in a terrible manner. In the early part of the xithcentury he was besieging here the Count of Anjou who had seized it, when he heard the defenders shouting from the top of the ramparts " Skins ! Skins ! " At this time he was only the Bastard, and his mother was a tanner's daughter. The garrison of the besieged city were jeering at him by imitating his grandfather, the tanner crying his wares. In order to teach them that it was not good for them to make fun of his illegitimate descent from a commoner, Duke William had the hands

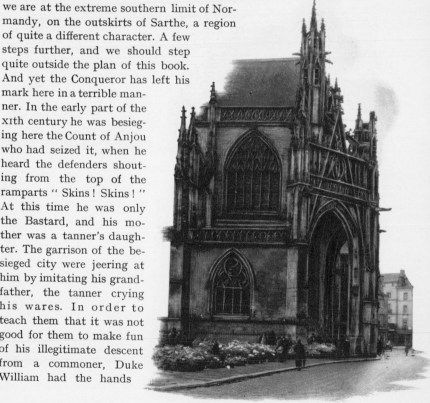

Alençon. The Cathedral.

and feet of thirty prisoners cut off and thrown at them, promising them all a like fate; and this shower of bleeding limbs so terrified the men of Alençon that they humbly surrendered to the fierce duke. Alençon, watered by the Sarthe and the Briante, surrounded by pleasant country, an appanage of the royal house of France since the days of the

Alençon. The Château.

Valois, is a healthy and attractive town. Its church of Notre-Dame, with its magnificent flamboyant doorway and the stone lace-work of its aisles, was to a large extent spoilt by a false classicism in the xviiith century. The house known as the Maison d'Ozé is a charming type of a xvth century pleasure-house; the demolished castle can still show a fortified gate and a tower of the most war-like appearance; and in the museum are to be found remarkable canvasses by Jouvenet, Chardin, Vigée-Lebrun, Largillière, Courbet, Delacroix, Boudin, Jean-Paul Laurens. But the best pictures remain those which are painted by Nature : if we visit Saint-Léonard-des-Bois, Fresnay, or Saint-Céneri, where there are Romanesque chapels dedicated to pious hermits, or venture into the mysterious Forest of Perseigne, a true home of legends and fairy apparitions, we shall enjoy the most refined pleasures which " Sweet France " can offer her faithful admirers.

Soligny.

At Mortagne we are in the Perche; and though administrative conventions have placed this town in the department of Orne, the soul of

Monastery of Soligny.
La Trappe.

Normandy is no longer here, in this old " Mauritania " which has nothing remarkable to offer; but which, perched on a hill, was made into a fortress to its undoing. Few towns have been more often taken and re-taken : once by the Capets, twice by the English, and twenty-two times during the age of the League — a sinister record. Not far from Mortagne is Bellevue, another fortress of olden days predestined to tragedy. It was the fief of that Robert of Bellevue who built a number of fortresses throughout the whole of this region in the xIth century, and to whom is attributed even that of Gisors. He was the Vauban of his time, and the most celebrated member of a family of redoubtable tyrants who managed to get the whole of the Perche into their hands, from Alençon to Nogent-le-Rotrou. To the north of Mortagne, at Soligny-la-Trappe, is the tomb of the Abbé de Rancé, round

Verneuil. Church of the Magdalen.

which float the austere memories of the famous order of the Trappists, and of the monastery of which the original oratory was founded in the middle of the xiith century by Rotrou, Count of Le Perche. This was a result of the disaster of the White Ship, which had gone down off Barfleur, with the royal family of England and a host of Anglo-Norman lords and their wives on board. The abbey underwent many vicissitudes. Rancé reformed it and reorganised it when, in consequence of a terrible tragedy of love and death, he took refuge in an exalted ardour of religion. The Revolution overthrew all the old buildings. Those which one visits now are modern, and the monks have had to give way to a well-known chocolate manufactory. But the soul of this mother-house of the Trappists remains none the less unimpaired in these grave and beautiful surroundings.

Nothing much else will be found but Laigle — with its flamboyant church of St. Martin and its château built by Mansart — before reaching Verneuil on the outskirts of the Forest of Breteuil by way of the valley of the Risle. This will be the last Norman city before the end of our journey; but it will leave us some very interesting memories by way of farewell. Verneuil is another example of those deserted towns, fallen from their former state and crushed beneath the weight of a great past, which one often meets with in Normandy. It was created as a complete whole by Henry I of England, who desired to make it one of his chief strongholds on the frontiers of the Ile-de-France. After the conquest of Normandy by Philip Augustus, Verneuil became French, and remained so; but during the Hundred Years' War the En-

Verneuil. Notre-Dame.

glish inflicted a crushing defeat upon one of Charles VII's armies, which restored the town to the " Godons" ("God damns", i. e. the English) till the appearance of Joan of Arc. The storming of Verneuil in 1449 once more made it a city of the Kings of France. It was to witness a last tragedy at the execution of the royalist Frotté in 1800. Then came a process of gradual depopulation, ending in silence. Verneuil, built between the Aure and a branch of the Itou, has still its old houses, its ramparts planted with limes, the church of La Madeleine, whose

Château d'O.

flamboyant tower is one of the most striking in the whole of Normandy, the Romanesque and Gothic church of Notre-Dame, very much spoilt, and the Tour Grise, a XIIth century keep disfigured by the whims of a sorry archaeologist. The surroundings of Verneuil are pretty, extending as far as the Forest of Breteuil, which is very long, and leads, with scarcely a break, to that of Conches and the outskirts of Evreux. Our circuit is now complete. We have travelled round Normandy, trying to follow, in this southern region, an administrative frontier which is often artificial, and a natural frontier which is often indistinguishable; for the continuations of Armorica, and the encroachments of the regions of Mayenne, Sarthe, Eure and Loire, make it hard to appreciate exactly at what point Normandy takes its rise in the basins of the Loire and the Seine in order to achieve its magnificent bloom in the direction of the sea. But below the surface of official subdivision, so often changed under various governments, lies the everlasting history of the soil and the race. And in Normandy the narrative is sufficiently complex, as indeed it is in most of these provinces whose fields have been the cockpit of warring factions. Within the compass of this book we realise that it is impossible to define what we may term " l'idée normande ". The history of Normandy is made up of Danish and Baltic Vikings, Angles, the people of the Ile-de-France, of the Maine, of the Perche, and of Brittany, of Angevins, pagans, catholics, protestants, royalists and revolutionaries. And it is the secret of Normandy that she has welded together into one whole these discordant elements born of the soil and of the sea. Patriotism and religion have been the most potent factors in this apparent miracle, and they have stood the test of the most deadly ordeals. How much may be read into the famous Norman maxim, at once stubborn and litigious " It is my right and I hold to it ". And it is just because she has felt her prescriptive rights and has maintained them with infinite patience that Normandy has resisted successfully innumerable attacks and appears to us as a radiant unity in her place among the lovely provinces of France.

A Normandy Market.

A Normandy Landscape.

CHAPTER X

—

The Land — Feudal — Humanist and Christian

We have made the circuit of Normandy both by land and sea. We have also traversed it inland, following the ridges of its hills and its river-arteries. But how many of its beauties we have forgotten! And how is one to express the soul of a country — that invisible element which is everything, since it is the emotion and the love arising from things seen.

History, evoked by the hasty glances we have cast upon abbeys, castles and cathedrals, has been able to teach us but little of its great lesson, which shows the oblivious present to what extent the past remains essential and living. But it has perhaps an even more efficacious lesson. It is born of the configuration of a village, hiding in a hollow valley or in a cleft in the rock. Here it is expressed in the grey stone of a neighbourhood with roofs of bluish slate; there in the thatched cottages, calling up visions of primitive mediaeval poverty; and in yet another place, where stone is scarce and wood abundant, it is expressed in the sturdy frames of oak

or beech, with their interstices filled with white rough-cast; yet again it
is seen in brick blackened by time, like a burnt-out fire-brand. A pleasant
church in no particular style may sometimes appear as moving as the
spire of a superb flamboyant cathedral; and down on the level plains of
wheat, the fine openwork spires of the Norman bell-towers sum up in
themselves the whole character of the place and people. It finds expression
in the murmur of the sea-winds which rustle across the plateaux of Caux
or in the walled farms of the Cotentin, or across the mysterious heath of
Lessay. The intense green of the pastures of the Avranchin and the Vexin
are the very symbol of fertility; and the numberless cows, with the chan-
ging silken gleam of their coats — amber, deep russet or tawny with a
silver tinge — seem as it were set fast in a flow of molten emerald. It is
enchanting to wander beneath the light arching foliage of the apple-
orchards of the Virois or the district of Auge. The sky between the inter-
lacing boughs appears as it were like fruits of blue light mingled with the
ruddy or golden apples, whose excessive abundance bends the laden
branches earthwards; and in the spring-time, when the pink and white
blossoms gleam like a fairy vision, all is fragrant among the patches of
sunlight. There are orchards where one suddenly realises the eternal
youth expressed in the word " Virgilian ". It is good to linger over one's
happy fortune when one comes upon these markets full of magnificent
beasts, with their rich colour worthy of Jordaens, where, amidst the
mooing of kine and the neighing of horses, the clinking of glasses and the
cracking of whips, the peasants in their shining blouses group themselves
round their open-air kitchens. One should dream on the great cliffs
before the charge of the sea-horses, or loiter on the end of the jetty in
some little port at the hour when the fishing-boats are coming home,
lowering their sails, while the lights are coming out and the moon is
rising. One should watch some lace-maker in a courtyard, under a
granite porch, weaving her countless bobbins with gentle patience, as in
the picture by Vermeer; or watch at the edge of the high-road the
passage of the pretty Norman carts, so jaunty, so rapid and so well-sprung,
full of people looking like characters out of Maupassant; or, like a weary
pedestrian intoxicated with the breeze as it passes over the sea or the
cornfields, seek a comfortable inn at the edge of a wood. I have not had
space to tell of all this; and yet it is this above all of which one should
tell, for it is this that makes one love a country.

Normandy makes one happy because it is happy itself. It well
deserves to be, for it has suffered greatly. What crimes have been com-
mitted by men in order to possess it ! It has seen marching down its roads

the red-haired Vikings with their bronze axes, William's trusty men with their coats of chain-armour, the English archers with their cross-bows and red tunics, the heavy-armed men-at-arms of Dunois and the Maid, the shield-bearers of Philip Augustus and Richard Cœur-de-Lion, the vanquished armies of Verneuil and the victors of Formigny, the Huguenots of Montgomery and the Leaguers of Mayenne and Matignon, the Gascons who followed Henry IV and the Chouans who rallied round Frotté; and all these were fierce warriors who hanged and pillaged the wretched inhabitants. And Normandy was brave, patient and faithful to the Kings at Paris to whom it had yielded. After every fresh act of pillage, Normandy restored its ruined houses, set to work again and trusted to its soil. It has been constant and prudent, subtle but loyal. It has had small time for dreams. It has been the land of faith, duty, law and reason, of the sense of law and the critical sense; and all this has enabled it to bear up against its hard fate as a much-coveted province, and reach its full development in the glorious peace which it now enjoys.

It has given France a fine crop of men of talent and genius. At Les Andelys, Nicolas Poussin; at Rouen, Pierre Corneille and his brother, Jouvenet, the Champmeslé, Guy de la Brosse, Fontenelle, Géricault, Flaubert; at Bayeux, Alain Chartier and Arcisse de Caumont; at Caen, Malherbe; at Saint-Lô, Le Verrier; at Le Havre, Bernardin de Saint-Pierre, Casimir Delavigne, Frederick Lemaître; at Saint-Sauveur-le-Vicomte, Barbey d'Aurevilly; at Fécamp, Jean Lorrain; at Miromesnil, Guy de Maupassant; at Coutances, Remy de Gourmont; at Valognes, Leopold Delisle, Burnouf, Dacier; at Honfleur, Le Play, Albert Sorel, Eugène Boudin, Henri de Régnier; at Le Bocage, Richard Lenoir; at Pont-l'Evêque, Admiral Hamelin; at Gruchy in the Cotentin, François Millet; besides a hundred more; geologists like Elie de Beaumont; poets or imaginative writers like Bois-Robert, Saint-Amand, Segrais, Charles-Théophile Feret; scholars like Siméon Luce or Léon Gautier; sculptors like the brothers Anguier; jurists like Demolombe; mathematicians like Laplace; surgeons like Tillaux; moralists like St. Evremond; painters like Théodule Ribot or Léandre; intrepid corsairs and explorers, great builders of ships or castles, captains of industry, priors, legists, high-hearted citizens, faithful adherents of the fine law-courts and the sove-reign cathedral; all steeped in law, lovers of logic and proportion, inde-pendent but disciplined, upheld by that framework of good sense which, in really intellectual natures, is the underlying condition of lasting work. It has given us a brilliant series of historians; story-tellers of the highest order, who have observed a classic restraint even in the most violent naturalism; a few fine painters and some local colourists who are too little appreciated. Music alone has left Normandy almost indifferent. The land of Corneille, Malherbe, Flaubert and Géricault can offer, among musicians, none but Boieldieu and Auber. But architecture, the domain of noble, unknown artists, balked of well-merited renown, has found in this land of Normandy a host of marvellous workers in stone; for architecture is the art which unites the maximum of imagination and inner aspiration with the highest demands on the reason; and Normandy is the home of reason, where one may almost say that the whole land, both its landscapes and its inhabitants, form one of those old " books of reason ", lying open to the sky in the heart of nature.

It is this which has given it its resisting power. The ancient invasions have been succeeded by the peaceful invasions of to-day, that of vulgarising tourists, of the fashion for sea-bathing, which destroys the character of the coasts; of the railways and factories, which do away with local idiosyncrasies and drain away the country labourers into the industrial cities, leaving old trades deserted, ancient customs obliterated, and the usages and costumes of olden days turned to ridicule in favour of unhealthy habits and far more ridiculous dresses; and lastly alcoholism. It cannot be denied that Normandy has been a little shaken by these simultaneous attacks of " progress ", that destroyer of provincial traditions. Queen among lace-makers, with her fairy-like creations of Alençon, Argentan, Caen and Bayeux, she has seen this exquisite art perish, and laborious efforts are being made to revive it. No more are those astonishing confections of open-work stitchery constructed which crowned the heads of its women, recalling the lordly hennins of the Middle Ages. With the disappearance of the long evenings at home, legends have faded, folk-lore has grown poorer, the old festivals and their customs have lost ground. A hateful gang has stripped the country dwelling-houses of their pottery and cupboards, which were so justly admired, but have become, like their spinning-wheels, museum pieces or ornaments of town-dwellers' homes. The regionalist movement has not been able to struggle against all this as successfully as might have been desired. But the horse and cattle-markets, where one sees those rich breeds of horses which are one of the glories of Normandy, have maintained all their picturesque activity, from Vire to Caen, from Saint-Lô to Alençon. And though the liqueur made from cider, and known as " Calvados ", has caused ravages among the race, for which the innocent apple and the healthy drink made from it cannot be held responsible, the tradition of plenteous family meals is not lost. The fairs have survived in spite of railway transport;

the motor has not replaced the cart. And no social propaganda will weaken devotion to the saints, the cult of the Virgin, assiduous attendance at sumptuous processions, faith in cures wrought by piety, respect for relics and for the dead, and — whatever may have been said of Norman avarice — generosity to the poor, in the affections of this sea-going race.

Normandy is a land of faith. It has proved this by devoting its best resources, from the xth century onwards, to multiplying on its soil those abbeys, basilicas and cathedrals whose number amazes us. It lavished its wealth and the genius of its architects has decked it with immortal adornments. We have admired these proofs of piety by dozens. But we have also forgotten them by dozens; and all Normandy bristles with belfries and spires. One stands amazed when one thinks that such a rich bloom was unfolded in the midst of the most troubled ages in history, among sieges, battles, pillage and fire. As a feudal land, Normandy has remained faithful to the liberties granted in her great Charter. A land of humanists, it has had a cult for law, and it was in its universities and abbeys that the strong traditions of Roman jurisprudence have been preserved and enriched. It was one of its sons who created the Chanson de Roland. It was another of them who wrote *Le Cid* and in *Polyeucte* and *Horace* blended nationalism with logic and an aspiration towards the highest things.

And lastly, it is a Christian land, rather than a specifically Catholic one. Even nowadays, our observation of its opinions and customs shows us that the Norman, pious though he may be, is hardly clerical, and does not care for those whose kingdom is not of this world to interfere in the guidance of his own. No conversion was more spontaneous and sincere than that of the old pirates who were suffered to organise their conquest as a duchy. It was with equal loyalty of heart and spirit that Normandy gave itself to Jesus and still more, perhaps, to the Virgin, as it did to the Kings of France, after the great movement of conquest had gone over the sea to find a new fatherland. Nowhere have the clergy been more respected, better treated and favoured with greater fortune. And yet the Reformation met with immense sympathy on Norman soil. For the critical spirit and the passion for law were as strong as ever. Norman humour was never tired of mocking at the abuses and peccadilloes of the monks, and the civic spirit of the communes would not bow before the exactions of the bishops. The flaws of papal Rome in the xvith century — which had reverted to a semi-paganism, thanks to its intellectual passion for the Renaissance of the ancient world — were as displeasing to Norman moderation as was mediaeval asceticism. This moderation, abhorring all excess, this passion for legality and liberty, cost Normandy streams of blood; for, after being the battle-field of the French and English, it became that of the Leaguers and the Huguenots. But Protestant as it was in its liberalism, it has remained profoundly Christian. Thus it was accessible to the regionalism of the Girondins, to the federalist ideal, while remaining as recalcitrant to the fury of the Vendéans as to the Jacobin fanaticism, and never ceasing, even in its most violently separatist moments, to cherish the dream of a united France.

Liberty and faith, rational sanity, straightforward judgment, decision and prudence; these are the essence of the Norman soul, and nothing has changed it. It has become ardently attached to a fertile soil whose resources it has multiplied an hundred-fold by its genius for industry; through cultivation, stock-breeding, weaving and transport, fisheries and mines, the treasures on the surface of the land and beneath the soil. But over this land passes the great breath of the sea, the wind of adventure, as healthy as the sea salt. It will always mingle a touch of heroism with the grace of this country where life is so good. Idealism dominates everything, and even nowadays, when so many dogmas are moribund, its symbol is to be seen in the slender golden archangel aloft in the sky at the top of La Merveille, who chases away with his flaming sword alike the blind monsters of unbelief and the assaults of the ocean, terrible in its unconsciousness. Normandy is the favourite of its protector Saint-Michel-du-Péril.

Beach of Normandy.

INDEX

A

Agon, 105.
Aiguille de Belval, 46.
Ailly, 45.
Aire, 94.
Alençon, 16-17-128-140-142-143-145-152.
Allais, Alphonse, 66.
Amboise, Cardinals of, 19-54-58.
Andaine, 128-133-134.
Andelle, 23-31.
Andelys, Les, 16-17-20-22-23-151.
Ango, 40-42-43.
Anguier, 151.
Anjou, Count of, 142.
Antifer, 47.
Antony of Navarre, King, 22.
Aquitaine, 11.
Argentan, 17-128-140-152.
Arlette, 136-139.
Armorica, 103-111-147.
Arques, 12-34-35-37.

Arromanches, 78-94.
Arundel, Earl of, 32.
Asnelles, 94.
Auber, 152.
Auderville, 103.
Auge, 16-67-70-74-75-77-104-127-150.
Aumale, 35.
Aure, 147.
Aurigny, 104.
Avranches, 11-16-35-106-109-111-112-114-
    115-117-118-120-123-127-130-131-134.
Avranchin, 150.

B

Bagnoles, 128-134.
Barbès, 123.
Barbey d'Aurevilly, 106-108-151.
Barbizon, 138.
Barfleur, 98-145.
Bassano, 74.
Basselin, Olivier, 132.

Bathilde, 27.
Bavaria, Dukes of, 27.
Bayeux, 11-13-14-17-54-90-91-92-94-95-97-140-141-151-152.
Bazin, René, 106-131.
Beauce, 89.
Beaumont, 104.
Beaumont, Elie de, 151.
Beaumont-le-Roger, 69-71.
Bec-Hellouin, 68.
Bedford, Regent, 82.
Bellevue, 144.
Benedictines, 27-28-46-107-120.
Bénerville, 79.
Benouville, 46.
Béranger, 38.
Bernardin de Saint-Pierre, 62-151.
Bernay, 70.
Berneval, 42.
Bernières, 93.
Bernières, John of, 142.
Berry, Duchess of, 44.
Bessin, 11-16-89-92-94-127.
Biville-sur-Mer, 45.
Blanqui, 123.
Blois, Count of, 67.
Blondel, 56.
Blonville, 79.
Bocage, 13-16-127-131-136-138-151.
Boïeldieu, 152.
Boilly, 103.
Bois-Robert, 151.
Boissard de Boisdenier, 52.
Bonnières, 18.
Boudin, Eugène, 60-62-63-66-143-151.
Bourgtheroulde, Hôtel, 49-51-52.
Bray, 16-19-31-32-35.
Brèche au Diable, 140.
Brécy, 92.
Bresle, 35-37.
Brest, 95.
Breteuil, 146-147.
Briante, 143.
Brière, 77.
Brittany, 10-12-16-98-103-105-107-126-132-134.
Broglie, 70.
Brosse, Guy de la, 56-151.
Bruneval, 48.
Burnouf, 108-151.

C

Cabourg, 80-94.
Caen, 12-13-17-67-80-81-82-83-84-85-86-87-88-89-92-93-95-127-128-141-151-152.
Calvados, 16-67-83-92-95-152.

Camembert, 74.
Cancale, 111-117.
Cance, 16-128-129-130-131-134.
Carentan, 94.
Carpaccio, 88.
Carteret, 105.
Catherine de' Medici, 133.
Cauchon, Pierre, 72.
Caudebec, 29-57.
Caumont, Arcisse de, 80-151.
Caux, 9-10-11-16-17-29-31-37-38-39-40-43-44-65-90-127-150.
Chamblais, 70.
Champlain, Samuel de, 64.
Champmeslé, 56-151.
Chardin, 103-132-143.
Charlemagne, 27.
Charles VI, 50.
Charles VII, 12-19-22-27-147.
Charles the Bald, 20-22.
Charles the Bold, 35.
Charles the Simple, 11-18.
Charleval, 23.
Chartier, Alain, 151.
Chartres, 54.
Chateaubriand, 77-119.
Château-Gaillard, 20-21-22-23.
Cherbourg, 12-17-95-98-99-100-101-102-103-128.
Cima, 88.
Clécy, 89-128-135-136-138.
Clodion, 59-103.
Clotilde, Queen, 20.
Clovis II, 27.
Colbert, 12-24-58.
Coligny, 12.
Colombe, Michel, 19.
Compiègne, 36.
Conches, 68-69-128-147.
Condé-sur-Noireau, 128-135.
Constantius Chlorus, 109.
Corday, Charlotte, 13-74-82.
Corneille, 56-60-151-152.
Corot, 52-108-132-136.
Cosqueville, 98.
Côte de Grâce, 77.
Cotentin, 10-11-16-17-48-90-92-94-95-103-104-106-107-109-111-127-150-151.
Couesnon, 118-126.
Courbet, 52-60-88-143.
Courseulles, 93.
Coutainville, 105.
Coutances, 17-105-106-107-108-109-110-111-113-131-141-151.
Crevilly, Château de, 92-95.
Criel, 42.

Criquebœuf, 77-78.
Croisset, 24-27.

D

Dacier, 108-151.
Daubigny, 52-88-132-136.
David Gérard, 52.
Deauville, 78-79-104.
Delacroix, 52-143.
Delarue-Mardrus, Mme Lucie, 65.
Delavigne, Casimir, 62-151.
Delisle, Léopold, 108-151.
Demolombe, 151.
Denis, 64.
Diélette, 105.
Dieppe, 12-14-17-34-37-38-39-40-42-43-44-
   45-64-105-128.
Dives, 11-13-70-74-79-80-140.
Dol, 111.
Domfront, 16-17-35-127-128-132-133-134-
   136-138-142.
Dreux, 17.
Driant, Colonel, 32.
Duguesclin, 12-69-111.
Dumont d'Urville, 135.
Dunois, 50-151.
Duquesne, 44.
Durdent, 45.

E

Eaulne, 34.
Ecorches, 74.
Ecouves, 142.
Edward III of England, 64-82.
Edward the Confessor, 91.
Elbeuf, 24.
Eleanor of Aquitaine, 11-71.
Epte, 16-17-18-19-31.
Estrées, 95.
Etretat, 45-47-77-92-104.
Eu, 35-36-37.
Eure, 16-19-130-147.
Evreux, 12-16-17-67-68-69-70-128-147.

F

Falaise, 13-17-127-128-135-136-137-138-
   139-140.
Fécamp, 41-42-43-45-46-77-128-151.
Feret, Charles-Théophile, 151.
Fervacques, 74.
Feuillet, Octave, 108.
Flamanville, 105.
Flaubert, Gustave, 27-56-151-152.
Flers, 128.
Fleury, 23.
Fontaine-Henry, Château de, 88.

Fontenelle, 56-151.
Forain, 60.
Forges-les-Eaux, 32-36.
Formerie, 32.
Formigny, 12-82-94-151.
Fragonard, 74.
Francis I, 12-43-57.
Fredegond, 50.
Fremiet, 123.
Fresnay-sur-Sarthe, 141-143.
Frotté, 147-151.

G

Gaillon, 19.
Gatteville, 98.
Gautier, Léon, 151.
Genêts, 106-117-118.
Geoffrey Plantagenet, 71.
Gerberoy, 32-33.
Géricault, 52-55-56-60-151-152.
Ghirlandajo, 103.
Gisors, 16-18-19-31-139-144.
Giverny, 18.
Goujon, Jean, 55.
Gourmont, Remy de, 111-134-151.
Gournay, 16-31.
Goyen, Van, 52-118.
Grand Bé, 119.
Grandcamp, 94.
Granville, 17-77-105-106-117-128.
Greuze, 103.
Gréville, 104-105.
Gruchy, 104-151.
Guiscard, 11.
Guiscard, Robert, 14.
Guises, 36.

H

Hamelin, Admiral, 66-151.
Harfleur, 12-29-30-57.
Harold, 11-35-91-139.
Hastings, Battle of, 11-91.
Henry I of England, 34-98-132-146.
Henry II of England, 11-69-71.
Henry IV, 12-19-22-34-35-38-58-69-151.
Henry V of England, 12-22-82.
Honfleur, 12-17-30-60-64-65-67-77-128-
   151.
Houlgate, 79.
Huet, Paul, 132.
Hugo, Victor, 29.
Hundred Years' War, 12-15-46-69-71-76-
   109-122-123-146.

I

Ile de France, 10-14-15-17-18-20-66-67-
   146.

Ile Lacroix, 56.
Ingres, 52-54.
Isabey, 47.
Isigny, 94.
Itou, 67-147.

J

James II of England, 95.
Joan of Arc, 12-36-50-56-72-147.
John Lackland, 22-67.
Jordaens, 150.
Jouvenet, 56-143-151.
Jullonville, 106.
Jumièges, 25-26-27-48.
Juste de Tours, 19.

K

Karr, Alphonse, 47.

L

La Bouille, 27.
La Hague, 77-96-100-102-103-104-107.
La Haye du Puits, 107.
La Hève, 48-57.
La Hire, 32.
La Hougue, 96, 100.
Laigle, 128-146.
Laize, 140.
La Londe, 27.
Lancaster, Duke of, 69.
Landemer, 104-105.
Lanfranc, 68.
Langrune, 78.
Laplace, 74-151.
Largillière, 52-143.
La Roche-Guyon, 18.
La Rochelle, 43.
La Roque, 30-76.
Laurens, Jean-Paul, 143.
Léandre, 151.
Le Brun, 87.
Le Havre, 12-17-29-30-39-45-48-57-58-59-60-62-63-64-66-78-93-151.
Le Neubourg, 68.
Lemaître, Frederick, 151.
Lenoir, Richard, 151.
Lépicié, 87.
Lépine, 88.
Le Play, 65-151.
Le Poittevin, 47.
Les Grandes Dalles, 45.
Les Petites Dalles, 45.
Le Sidaner, 32.
Lessay, 107-150.
Letourneur, 108.
Le Tréport, 16-37-39-42.

Le Verrier, 108-151.
Lieuvin, 16.
Lillebonne, 29-57.
Lion, 93.
Lisieux, 17-39-67-70-71-72-73-74-75-128.
Livarot, 74.
Loir, 130.
Loire, 147.
Lorrain, Jean, 46-151.
Louis Philippe, 36.
Louis VI (the Fat), 20.
Louis IX (the Saint) 34-122.
Louis XI, 12-122.
Louis XII, 51.
Louis XIV, 59.
Louis XVI, 58-100.
Louviers, 19-20.
Luc, 93.
Luce, Siméon, 151.
Lyons, Forest of, 23-31.

M

Mailloc, 74.
Malherbe, 83-151-152.
Manche, 16-131.
Mantes, 18-67.
Marat, 13-82.
Margaret of Burgundy, 22.
Matignon, 109-133-142-151.
Matilda, Queen, 35-81-88-90-99.
Maupassant, Guy de, 14-40-47-151.
Mayenne, Duke of, 34-37.
Mesnières, Château of, 31-34
Mesnil-Val, 42.
Meyerbeer, 138.
Mézeray, 140.
Mézidon, 74.
Millet, François, 104-105-151.
Miromesnil, 40-151.
Monet, Claude, 18-45-54-60-62.
Mont Camisy, 79.
Montgomery, 123-133-141-151.
Montivilliers, 46-48.
Montjoie, Rocks of, 130.
Montmartin, 105.
Mont Le Roule, 102.
Montmorency, 58.
Montmorency, Anne de, 88.
Montpensier, Mademoiselle de, 36.
Mont St. Michel, 11-16-17-77-106-110-112-114-115-117-118-119-121-122-124-125-126-127-130-154.
Morel-Fatio, 138.
Morny, Duc de, 78.
Morsalines, 95.
Mortagne, 128-144-145.

Mortain, 13-16-17-35-127-128-129-130-131-134-136.
Motelay, 138.

N

Nantes, Edict of, 12-24-44.
Napoleon, 99-100-102.
Neufbourg, 131.
Neufchâtel-en-Bray, 32-34-35.
Nez de Jobourg, 104.
Nogent-le-Rotrou, 145.
Normandy, Grail of, 46.
Nozal, 66.

O

Octeville, 48.
Oise, 32.
Omonville-la-Rogue, 103.
Orbec, 74.
Orne, 16-67-77-80-82-83-88-89-92-93-94-128-131-135-138-140-142-144.
Ouche, 16.
Ouistreham, 80-82-92.

P

Panini, 103.
Paris, 11-12-14-17-18-19-31-44-55-77-95.
Paynel, Jeanne, 110.
Perche, 16-130-144-145.
Périers, 107.
Perugino, 52-88.
Philip Augustus, 11-22-34-50-69-71-76-99-120-146-151.
Picardy, 16-31-37.
Pissarro, 60.
Pitres, 22-23-31.
Pointelin, 60.
Pont-Audemer, 76.
Pont-de-l'Arche, 20.
Pont-l'Evêque, 74-75-76-77-151.
Pontorson, 111-117.
Portbail, 105.
Port-en-Bessin, 77-94.
Pouchet, 56.
Pourbus, 103.
Pourville, 45.
Poussin, Nicolas, 103-108-132-151.
Puvis de Chavannes, 52.
Puys, 42.

Q

Quiberville, 45
Quillebœuf, 30-76.
Quinéville, 95.

R

Radepont, 23.
Rafaelli, 60.

Rame, 88.
Rancé, Abbé de, 145-146.
Régnéville, 105.
Régnier, Henri de, 65-151.
Renouf, 65.
Révolte des Nu-Pieds, 112.
Ribera, 103.
Ribot, Théodule, 65-151.
Richard Cœur-de-Lion, 20-54-151.
Richard I, 120.
Richelieu, 22-34-58.
Risle, 16-76-146.
Robert Curthose, 109-132.
Robert of Bellevue, 144.
Robert the Magnificent, 11-138-139.
Rollo, 11-13-18-31-35-50-81.
Rouen, 8-11-12-17-26-27-31-34-36-44-49-50-51-52-54-55-56-57-58-60-62-72-81-126-128-141-151.
Roumois, 16-26.
Rousseau, Theodore, 132-136.
Ruysdael, 52-74-118.

S

Saint-Adresse, 48-57-62.
Saint-Amand, 151.
Saint-André-d'Hébertot, 75.
St. Anselm, 68.
Saint Aubert, 112-120.
Saint-Aubin, 93.
Saint-Aubin-sur-Dun, 45.
Saint-Céneri, 141-143.
St. Clair, 18.
St. Columban, 28.
St. Evremond, 151.
St. Evroult, 11.
Saint-Exupère, 89.
Saint Front, 133.
St. Geneviève, 31.
Saint Germain, 11.
St. Honorin, 11.
Saint Jouin, 48.
Saint-Léonard, 116-117.
Saint-Léonard-des-Bois, 143.
Saint-Lô, 92-108-109-151-152.
St. Malo, 14-42-64-105-111-119-122.
Saint-Marcouf, 95.
St. Martin, 11.
St. Michael, 120.
St. Nicaise, 11.
Saint-Ouen, 11.
Saint-Pair, 11-106.
Saint Philibert, 27-48.
Saint Pierre Eglise, 98.
Saint-Pierre-en-Port, 45.
Saint-Sauveur-le-Vicomte, 108-151.

Saint-Taurin, 68.
Saint-Vaast, 77-95-96.
Saint-Valéry, 11-13-80.
Saint-Valéry-en-Caux, 45.
Saint-Valéry-sur-Somme, 45.
Saint-Wandrille, 11-24-26-27-28-30.
Salle, Cavalier de la, 56.
Sarthe, 16-130-142-143-147.
Scudérys, 62.
Sée, 16-111-115-118-134.
Séez, 138-141-142.
Segrais, 151.
Seine, 10-11-16-17-18-20-21-22-23-26-29-
    30-31-48-49-56-57-66-67-75-76-77-147.
Seine-Inférieure, 16-37.
Sélune, 16-118-134.
Seulle, 16-94.
Sohier, Hector, 84.
Soligny-la-Trappe, 144-145.
Somme, 16-37.
Sonneville, 45.
Sorel, Agnès, 27.
Sorel, Albert, 56-66-151.
Sully, 92.

T

Talbot, 50.
Tancarville, 30-66.
Tassaert, 88.
Tatihou, 95.
Tattegrain, 65.
Tesnières, 138.
Tessé-la-Madeleine, 135.
Thierry, Augustin, 86.
Thury-Harcourt, 128-135.
Tiepolo, 88.
Tillaux, 151.
Tinchebray, 132.
Tintoretto, 88.
Tombelaine, 117-119-122.
Torigny-sur-Vire, 109.
Touques, 16-70-74-77-78-79.
Trappists, 145-146.
Trouville, 77-78-79-94.
Troyon, 60-132.

U

Ussy, Vale of, 140.

V

Valognes, 106-107-108-109-151.
Van Dyck, 60.
Varangeville, 43-45.
Varaville, 80.
Varenne, 133-134.
Vauban, 95-100.
Vaucottes, 46.
Vauville, 110.
Vée, 134.
Verneuil, 16-128-145-146-147-151.
Vernier, 76.
Vernon, 18-31-82.
Veronese, 88.
Veules-les-Roses, 45.
Veulettes, 45.
Vexin, 14-16-31-150.
Vicq d'Azyr, 108.
Victoria, Queen, 36.
Vierville, 94.
Vigée-Lebrun, Madame, 52-143.
Villequier, 29.
Villers, 79.
Villerville, 77.
Vimeu, 35.
Vimoutiers, 74.
Vire, 16-17-94-127-130-131-132-135-152.
Virois, 104-150.

W

Wandrille, 28.
Weyden, Roger van der, 103.
White Ship, 98-145.
William Longsword, Duke, 54.
William of Alençon, 133.
William Rufus, 35-109.
William the Conqueror, 11-13-15-30-58-
    79-80-81-86-87-91-109-132-137-138-139-
    142-151.

Y

Yport, 46-47-48.
Yvetot, 38.

Z

Ziem, 52.